Level 1 • Part 1

Integrated Chinese

中文听说读写

WORKBOOK Simplified Characters

Third Edition

THIRD EDITION BY

Yuehua Liu and Tao-chung Yao
Nyan-Ping Bi, Yaohua Shi, Liangyan Ge

ORIGINAL EDITION BY

Tao-chung Yao and Yuehua Liu
Yea-fen Chen, Liangyan Ge,
Nyan-Ping Bi, Xiaojun Wang

CHENG & TSUI COMPANY
Boston

12th Printing, 2020

24 23 22 21 20   12 13 14 15 16

Published by
Cheng & Tsui Company, Inc.
25 West Street
Boston, MA 02111-1213 USA
Fax (617) 426-3669
www.cheng-tsui.com
"Bringing Asia to the World"™

ISBN 978-0-88727-640-8

Cover Design: studioradia.com

Cover Photographs: Man with map © Getty Images; Shanghai skyline © David Pedre/iStockphoto; Building with masks © Wu Jie; Night market © Andrew Buko. Used by permission.

Interior Design: Wanda España, Wee Design

Illustrations: 洋洋兔动漫

The *Integrated Chinese* series includes books, workbooks, character workbooks, audio products, multimedia products, teacher's resources, and more. Visit **www.cheng-tsui.com** for more information on the other components of *Integrated Chinese*.

Printed in the United States of America

Contents

Preface to the Third Edition

This new Workbook accompanies the third edition of *Integrated Chinese* (*IC*). In response to teachers' feedback and requests, the new *Integrated Chinese Level 1* includes 20 lessons (10 in Part 1 and 10 in Part 2), instead of 23 lessons as in the earlier editions. The format of the third edition Workbook remains largely unchanged. For maximum flexibility in pacing, each lesson is divided into two parts corresponding to the two sections of the lesson in the textbook. The exercises cover the language form and the four language skills of listening, speaking, reading, and writing.

We have also made several improvements and added new features in the new edition of the Workbook.

Three Modes of Communication Clearly Labeled

We would like to point out that our exercises cover the three modes of communication as explained in "Standards for Foreign Language Learning in the 21st Century": interpretive, interpersonal and presentational. We have labeled the exercises as interpretive, interpersonal or presentational wherever applicable.

More Authentic Materials Incorporated

To build a bridge between the pedagogical materials used in the classroom and the materials that the student will face in the target language environment, we have included authentic materials in the exercises for all lessons.

New Illustrations Added

To make the exercises more interesting and appealing, we have added many illustrations to the exercises. These visual images increase the variety of exercise types, and also stimulate the student to answer questions directly in Chinese without going through the translation process.

Contextualized Grammar Exercises and Task-Oriented Assignments Provided

The ultimate goal of learning any language is to be able to communicate in that language. With that goal in mind, we pay equal attention to language form and language function, and have created task-based exercises to train the student to handle real life situations using the language accurately and appropriately. We have rewritten many items, especially in the translation section, to provide linguistic context and to reflect the language used in real life.

Learner-Centered Tasks Included

We believe that the exercises in the Workbook should not only integrate the materials of the Textbook, but also relate to the student's life. We include exercises that simulate daily life with topics and themes that are relevant and personal to the student. We hope such open-ended exercises will actively engage students in the subject matter, and keep them interested in the language learning process. Since the world is constantly changing, we also have tried to add exercises that will train the student to meet the needs of today's world, such as writing e-mail messages in Chinese.

New Review Exercises Supplied

Every five lessons, a cumulative review unit is available to those students who wish to do a periodic progress check. The review units do not introduce any new learning materials, and can be included in or excluded from any curriculum planning, according to individual needs. These units are flexible, short, and useful as a review tool.

We would like to take this opportunity to thank all those who have given us feedback in the past, and extend our sincere gratitude to the two editors, Ying Yang of the University of California Berkeley and Zoe Wu of Pasadena City College, for their invaluable editorial comments and to Laurel Damashek at Cheng & Tsui for her support throughout the production process. We welcome your comments and feedback; please send any observations or suggestions to **editor@cheng-tsui.com.**

Preface to the Second Edition

In designing the Level One workbook exercises for *Integrated Chinese*, we strove to give equal emphasis to the students' listening, speaking, reading and writing skills. There are different difficulty levels in order to provide variety and flexibility to suit different curriculum needs. Teachers should assign the exercises at their discretion; they should not feel pressured into using all of them and should feel free to use them out of sequence, if appropriate. Moreover, teachers can complement this workbook with their own exercises.

The exercises in each lesson are divided into two parts. The exercises in Part One are for the first dialogue and those in Part Two are for the second dialogue. This way, the two dialogues in each lesson can be taught separately. The teacher can use the first two or three days to teach the first dialogue and ask the students to do all the exercises in Part One, then go on to teach the second dialogue. The teacher can also give the two separate vocabulary tests for the two dialogues so as to reduce the pressure of memorizing too many new words at the same time.

Listening Comprehension

All too often listening comprehension is sacrificed in a formal classroom setting because of time constraints. Students tend to focus their time and energy on the mastery of a few grammar points. This workbook tries to remedy this imbalance by including a substantial number of listening comprehension exercises. There are two categories of listening exercises; both can be done on the students' own time or in the classroom. In either case, it is important to have the instructor review the students' answers for accuracy.

The first category of listening exercises, which is at the beginning of this section, is based on the text of each lesson. For the exercises to be meaningful, students should *first* study the vocabulary list, and *then* listen to the recordings *before* attempting to read the texts. The questions are provided to help students' aural understanding of the texts and to test their reading comprehension.

The second category of listening exercises consists of an audio CD recording of two or more mini-dialogues or narratives. These exercises are designed to give students extra practice on the vocabulary and grammar points introduced in the lesson. Some of the exercises, especially ones that ask students to choose among several possible answers, are significantly more difficult than others. These exercises should be assigned towards the end of the lesson, when the students have become familiar with the content of the lesson.

Speaking Exercises

Here, too, there are two types of exercises. They are designed for different levels of proficiency within each lesson and should be assigned at the appropriate time.

To help students apply their newly-acquired vocabulary and grammatical understanding to meaningful communication, we first ask them questions related to the dialogues and narratives, and then ask them questions related to their own lives. These questions require a one- or two-sentence answer. By stringing together short questions and answers, students can construct their own mini-dialogues, practice in pairs or take turns asking or answering questions.

Once they have gained some confidence, students can progress to the more difficult questions, where they are invited to express opinions on a number of topics. Typically, these questions are abstract, so they gradually teach students to express their opinions in longer conversations. As the school year progresses, these types of questions should take up more class discussion time. Because this second type of speaking exercise is quite challenging, it should be attempted only *after* students are well grounded in the grammar and vocabulary of a particular lesson. Usually, this occurs *not immediately* after students have completed the first part of the speaking exercises.

Reading Comprehension

For the first seven lessons, the reading exercises appear in several different formats, including matching, translations, answering questions in English or answering multiple choice questions based on reading texts. There are also some authentic materials and modified authentic materials. Starting with Lesson 8, the format for reading exercises is fi xed. Th e first section of the lesson asks questions based on the dialogues in the textbook. Th e second section offers several reading passages with questions that are relevant to the themes of the current lesson.

Writing and Grammar Exercises

Grammar and Usage

These drills and exercises are designed to solidify students' grasp of important grammar points. Through brief exchanges, students answer questions using specific grammatical forms, or are given sentences to complete. Because they must provide context for these exercises, students cannot treat them as simple mechanical repetition drills.

In the last three lessons, students are introduced to increasingly sophisticated and abstract vocabulary. Corresponding exercises help them to grasp the nuances of new words. For example, synonyms are a source of great difficulty, so exercises are provided to help students distinguish between them.

Translation

Translation has been a tool for language teaching throughout the ages, and positive student feedback confirms our belief that it continues to play an important role. The exercises we have devised serve to reinforce two primary areas: one, to get students to apply specific grammatical structures; and two, to allow students to build their ever-increasing vocabulary. Ultimately, our hope is that this dual-pronged approach will enable students to understand that it takes more than just literal translation to convey an idea in a foreign language.

Writing Practice

This is the culmination of the written exercises, and it is where students learn to express themselves in writing. Many of the topics overlap with those used in oral practice. We expect that students will find it easier to put in writing what they have already learned to express orally.

Introduction

Pronunciation Exercises

I. Single Syllable

Listen carefully and circle the correct answer.

A. Simple Finals

1. **a.** bā   **b.** bū
2. **a.** kē   **b.** kā
3. **a.** gū   **b.** gē
4. **a.** pū   **b.** pō
5. **a.** lú   **b.** lǘ

B. Initials

1. **a.** pà   **(b.)** bà
2. **(a.)** pí   **b.** bí
3. **a.** nán   **(b.)** mán
4. **(a.)** fú   **b.** hú
5. **a.** tīng   **(b.)** dīng
6. **(a.)** tǒng   **b.** dǒng
7. **(a.)** nán   **b.** lán
8. **a.** niàn   **(b.)** liàn
9. **a.** gàn   **(b.)** kàn
10. **(a.)** kuì   **b.** huì
11. **a.** kǎi   **(b.)** hǎi
12. **a.** kuā   **(b.)** huā

13. **a.** jiān   **b.** qiān
14. **a.** yú   **b.** qú
15. **a.** xiāng   **b.** shāng
16. **a.** chú   **b.** rú
17. **a.** zhá   **b.** zá
18. **a.** zì   **b.** cì
19. **a.** sè   **b.** shè
20. **a.** sè   **b.** cè
21. **a.** zhǒng   **b.** jiǒng
22. **a.** shēn   **b.** sēn
23. **a.** rù   **b.** lù
24. **a.** xiào   **b.** shào
25. **a.** qì   **b.** chì

C. Compound Finals

1. **a.** tuō   **b.** tōu
2. **a.** guǒ   **b.** gǒu
3. **a.** duò   **b.** dòu
4. **a.** diū   **b.** dōu
5. **a.** liú   **b.** lóu
6. **a.** yǒu   **b.** yǔ
7. **a.** nǔ   **b.** nǚ
8. **a.** lú   **b.** lǘ
9. **a.** yuán   **b.** yán
10. **a.** píng   **b.** pín
11. **a.** làn   **b.** luàn
12. **a.** huán   **b.** hán
13. **a.** fèng   **b.** fèn
14. **a.** bèng   **b.** bèn
15. **a.** lún   **b.** léng
16. **a.** bīn   **b.** bīng
17. **a.** kěn   **b.** kǔn

18.	**a.** héng	**b.** hóng
19.	**a.** téng	**b.** tóng
20.	**a.** kēng	**b.** kōng
21.	**a.** pàn	**b.** pàng
22.	**a.** fǎn	**b.** fǎng
23.	**a.** mín	**b.** míng
24.	**a.** pēn	**b.** pān
25.	**a.** rén	**b.** rán

D. Tones: First and Fourth (Level and Falling)

1.	**a.** bō	**b.** bò
2.	**a.** pān	**b.** pàn
3.	**a.** wù	**b.** wū
4.	**a.** tà	**b.** tā
5.	**a.** qū	**b.** qù
6.	**a.** sì	**b.** sī
7.	**a.** fēi	**b.** fèi
8.	**a.** duì	**b.** duī
9.	**a.** xià	**b.** xiā
10.	**a.** yā	**b.** yà

E. Tones: Second and Third (Rising and Low)

1.	**a.** mǎi	**b.** mái
2.	**a.** fǎng	**b.** fáng
3.	**a.** tú	**b.** tǔ
4.	**a.** gé	**b.** gě
5.	**a.** wú	**b.** wǔ
6.	**a.** bǎ	**b.** bá
7.	**a.** zhǐ	**b.** zhí
8.	**a.** huǐ	**b.** huí
9.	**a.** féi	**b.** fěi
10.	**a.** láo	**b.** lǎo

F. Tones: All Four Tones

1. **a.** bà   **b.** bā
2. **a.** pí   **b.** pì
3. **a.** méi   **b.** měi
4. **a.** wēn   **b.** wěn
5. **a.** zǎo   **b.** zāo
6. **a.** yōu   **b.** yóu
7. **a.** guāng   **b.** guǎng
8. **a.** cí   **b.** cǐ
9. **a.** qì   **b.** qí
10. **a.** mào   **b.** máo
11. **a.** bǔ   **b.** bù
12. **a.** kuàng   **b.** kuāng
13. **a.** jú   **b.** jǔ
14. **a.** qiáng   **b.** qiāng
15. **a.** xián   **b.** xiān
16. **a.** yǒng   **b.** yòng
17. **a.** zú   **b.** zū
18. **a.** suī   **b.** suí
19. **a.** zhèng   **b.** zhēng
20. **a.** chòu   **b.** chóu
21. **a.** shuāi   **b.** shuài
22. **a.** wǒ   **b.** wò
23. **a.** yào   **b.** yáo
24. **a.** huī   **b.** huì
25. **a.** rú   **b.** rù

G. Comprehensive Exercise

1. **a.** jiā   **b.** zhā
2. **a.** chuí   **b.** qué
3. **a.** chǎng   **b.** qiǎng
4. **a.** xū   **b.** shū

 5. **a.** shuǐ   **b.** xuě

 6. **a.** zǎo   **b.** zhǎo

 7. **a.** zǎo   **b.** cǎo

 8. **a.** sōu   **b.** shōu

 9. **a.** tōu   **b.** tuō

 10. **a.** dǒu   **b.** duǒ

 11. **a.** duǒ   **b.** zuǒ

 12. **a.** mǎi   **b.** měi

 13. **a.** chóu   **b.** qiú

 14. **a.** yuè   **b.** yè

 15. **a.** jiǔ   **b.** zhǒu

 16. **a.** nǔ   **b.** nǚ

 17. **a.** zhú   **b.** jú

 18. **a.** jì   **b.** zì

 19. **a.** liè   **b.** lüè

 20. **a.** jīn   **b.** zhēn

 21. **a.** xiǔ   **b.** shǒu

 22. **a.** kǔn   **b.** hěn

 23. **a.** shǎo   **b.** xiǎo

 24. **a.** zhǎng   **b.** jiǎng

 25. **a.** qū   **b.** chū

II. Tone Combination Exercise

Name that "tone": You will hear one word at a time. Write down the tones in the blank. Use 1-4 for the four tones, and 5 for neutral tones.

EXAMPLE: If you hear the word "Zhōngwén," you write <u>"1 2"</u> on the blank.

A.

1. <u>Měi guó</u>
   3 2

2. <u>hán gúo</u>
   2 2

3. <u>xībáiyá</u>
   1 1 2

4. <u>fēitī</u>

5. <u>dì tián</u>

6. <u>chūzōtìchú</u>
   4 4 4

7. <u>xiāng zhǎo</u>
   1 1

8. <u>píngúo</u>
   2 3

9. <u>tào méi</u>
   3 2

10. <u>chēn shēn</u>
    4 1

11. <u>lǐng dǎi</u>
    3 4

12. <u>nìo zǎi kù</u>
    2 3 4

B. Multisyllabic Words

1. _____	11. _____	21. _____
2. _____	12. _____	22. _____
3. _____	13. _____	23. _____
4. _____	14. _____	24. _____
5. _____	15. _____	25. _____
6. _____	16. _____	26. _____
7. _____	17. _____	27. _____
8. _____	18. _____	28. _____
9. _____	19. _____	29. _____
10. _____	20. _____	30. _____

III. Initials and Simple Finals

Fill in the blanks with appropriate initials or simple finals.

A.1.	_b_a	**A.2.**	p_o_	**A.3.**	_m_u	**A.4.**	l_i_
B.1.	f_o_	**B.2.**	n_a_	**B.3.**	_p_i	**B.4.**	_b_u
C.1.	_p_a	**C.2.**	l_e_	**C.3.**	l_ü_	**C.4.**	_h_u
D.1.	_d_u	**D.2.**	t_e_	**D.3.**	n_u_	**D.4.**	n_ü_
E.1.	_k_e	**E.2.**	_g_u	**E.3.**	_h_a		
F.1.	g_e_	**F.2.**	k_u_	**F.3.**	h_e_		
G.1.	_ch_u	**G.2.**	_j_i	**G.3.**	_x_u		
H.1.	j_u_	**H.2.**	q_i_	**H.3.**	x_i_		
I.1.	_t_a	**I.2.**	_z_e	**I.3.**	_s_i	**I.4.**	_zh_u
J.1.	_s_u	**J.2.**	c_e_	**J.3.**	_z_u	**J.4.**	_x_i
K.1.	_z_i	**K.2.**	s_ü_	**K.3.**	_t_a	**K.4.**	q_u_
L.1.	_z_a	**L.2.**	_zh_i	**L.3.**	s_u_	**L.4.**	_ch_u
M.1.	c_i_	**M.2.**	_q_i	**M.3.**	_sh_u	**M.4.**	_j_a
N.1.	_sh_u	**N.2.**	r_u_	**N.3.**	ch_i_	**N.4.**	_r_e

IV. Tones

Listen to the audio and mark the correct tone marks.

A.1.	he	**A.2.**	ma	**A.3.**	pa	**A.4.**	di
B.1.	nü	**B.2.**	re	**B.3.**	chi	**B.4.**	zhu
C.1.	mo	**C.2.**	qu	**C.3.**	ca	**C.4.**	si
D.1.	tu	**D.2.**	fo	**D.3.**	ze	**D.4.**	ju
E.1.	lü	**E.2.**	bu	**E.3.**	xi	**E.4.**	shi
F.1.	gu	**F.2.**	se	**F.3.**	ci	**F.4.**	ku
G.1.	mang	**G.2.**	quan	**G.3.**	yuan	**G.4.**	yue
H.1.	yi	**H.2.**	er	**H.3.**	san	**H.4.**	si
I.1.	ba	**I.2.**	qi	**I.3.**	liu	**I.4.**	wu
J.1.	jiu	**J.2.**	shi	**J.3.**	tian	**J.4.**	jin
K.1.	mu	**K.2.**	shui	**K.3.**	huo	**K.4.**	ren
L.1.	yu	**L.2.**	zhuang	**L.3.**	qun	**L.4.**	zhong

V. Compound Finals

Fill in the blanks with compound finals.

1. a. zhái   **1. b.** tān   **1. c.** kuen   **1. d.** jeng

2. a. xien   **2. b.** qia   **2. c.** jun   **2. d.** doa

3. a. xia   **3. b.** zhen   **3. c.** tao   **3. d.** gong

4. a. shuai   **4. b.** biao   **4. c.** zai   **4. d.** quen

5. a. jiao   **5. b.** dian   **5. c.** xin   **5. d.** chang

6. a. zhun   **6. b.** liung   **6. c.** kua   **6. d.** jiang

7. a. sue   **7. b.** xue   **7. c.** pao   **7. d.** chuang

VI. Compound Finals and Tones

Fill in the blanks with compound finals and mark the appropriate tone marks.

1. a. máng   **1. b.** zhuā   **1. c.** shuě   **1. d.** zhuāng

2. a. shái   **2. b.** tǎng   **2. c.** liàn   **2. d.** bāo

3. a. sǔng   **3. b.** juě   **3. c.** kǎi   **3. d.** dàn

4. a. luǎn   **4. b.** qià   **4. c.** tuǎ   **4. d.** xióng

5. a. fǎo   **5. b.** pèng   **5. c.** xún   **5. d.** jūn

6. a. běn   **6. b.** jiǎo   **6. c.** qià   **6. d.** tiáo

7. a. lín   **7. b.** guǎi   **7. c.** quěn   **7. d.** xiǎng

VII. Neutral Tones

Name that "tone": You will hear one word at a time. Write down the tones in the blanks. Use the numbers 1–4 for the four tones, and 5 for neutral tones.

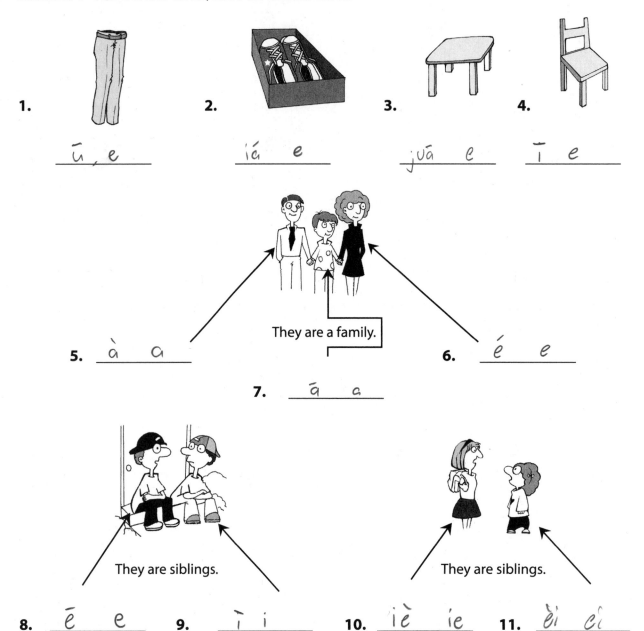

1. _____ū____e_____

2. _____iá____e_____

3. ____juā____e_____

4. _____ī____e_____

They are a family.

5. _____à____a_____

6. _____é____e_____

7. _____á____a_____

They are siblings.

8. _____é____e_____

9. _____ī____i_____

They are siblings.

10. ____iè____ie_____

11. ____èi____cî_____

VIII. Exercises on Initials, Finals, and Tones: Disyllabic Words

Put the letter of what you hear into the parentheses.

( ) **1.**   **a.**   làoshī   **b.**   lǎoshī   **c.**   lǎoshí   teacher

( ) **2.**   **a.**   nǔ'ér   **b.**   nǔ'èr   **c.**   nǔ'ér   daughter

( ) **3.**   **a.**   zhàopiàn   **b.**   zhāopiàn   **c.**   zháopiàn   photograph

( ) **4.** **a.** wànfàn   **b.** wǎnfān   **c.** wǎnfàn   dinner
( ) **5.** **a.** shēngrì   **b.** shéngrì   **c.** shěngrì   birthday
( ) **6.** **a.** zāijiàn   **b.** zàijiàn   **c.** záijiàn   goodbye
( ) **7.** **a.** xuéshēng   **b.** xuèsheng   **c.** xuésheng   student
( ) **8.** **a.** diànyǐng   **b.** diānyǐng   **c.** diànyìng   movie
( ) **9.** **a.** zuòtiān   **b.** zuótiān   **c.** zuótiàn   yesterday
( ) **10.** **a.** suírán   **b.** suīrán   **c.** suīràn   although
( ) **11.** **a.** xièxiè   **b.** shèshe   **c.** xièxie   thanks
( ) **12.** **a.** kāfēi   **b.** káfēi   **c.** kāifēi   coffee
( ) **13.** **a.** kēlè   **b.** kělè   **c.** kělà   cola
( ) **14.** **a.** píngcháng   **b.** pēngchán   **c.** píngchèng normally
( ) **15.** **a.** gōngzuò   **b.** gōngzhuò   **c.** gōngzòu   work
( ) **16.** **a.** piàoliàng   **b.** piāoliang   **c.** piàoliang beautiful
( ) **17.** **a.** wèntì   **b.** wèntí   **c.** wěntí   questions
( ) **18.** **a.** rōngyì   **b.** lóngyì   **c.** róngyì   easy
( ) **19.** **a.** kāishǐ   **b.** kāixǐ   **c.** kāisǐ   begin
( ) **20.** **a.** loùdiǎn   **b.** liùdiǎn   **c.** liùdǎn   six o'clock

IX. Exercises on Initials, Finals, and Tones: Monosyllabic Words

Transcribe what you hear into *pinyin* with tone marks.

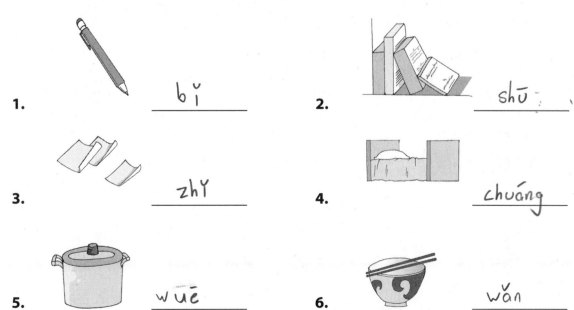

1. _____ bǐ _____

2. _____ shū _____

3. _____ zhǐ _____

4. _____ chuáng _____

5. _____ wūé _____

6. _____ wǎn _____

7. _qián_

8. _gǎo_

9. _māo_

10. _yáng_

11. _niú_

12. _shé_

X. Exercises on Initials, Finals, and Tones: Cities

Listen to the *pinyin* words in the left column and identify the cities they represent.

EXAMPLE: Mài'āmì → Miami

(c)	1.	Bōshìdùn	a.	Venice
(h)	2.	Lúndūn	b.	Toronto
(f)	3.	Niǔyuē	c.	Boston
(g)	4.	Bālí	d.	Chicago
(d)	5.	Zhījiāgē	e.	Seattle
(i)	6.	Běijīng	f.	New York
(j)	7.	Luòshānjī	g.	Paris
(b)	8.	Duōlúnduō	h.	London
(e)	9.	Xīyǎtú	i.	Beijing
(a)	10.	Wēinísī	j.	Los Angeles

XI. Exercises on Initials, Finals, and Tones: Countries

Transcribe what you hear into *pinyin* with tone marks and identify what countries they are.

EXAMPLE: <u>Rìběn</u>   →   <u>Japan</u>

1. _____   →   _____

2. _____   →   _____

3. _____   →   _____

4. _____   →   _____

5. _____   →   _____

6. _____   →   _____

7. _____   →   _____

8. _____   →   _____

9. _____   →   _____

10. _____   →   _____

 ## XII. Exercises on Initials, Finals, and Tones: American Presidents

Transcribe what you hear into pinyin with tone marks and identify which American presidents they are.

1. _____   →   _____

2. _____   →   _____

3. _____   →   _____

4. _____   →   _____

5. _____   →   _____

6. _____   →   _____

7. _____   →   _____

8. _____   →   _____

9. _____   →   _____

10. _____   →   _____

急 诊 室
JI ZHEN SHI

The tones for the three characters on the sign are 2, 3, and 4. Can you pronounce what's on the sign? If you can, then you know how to say "emergency room" in Chinese.

LESSON 1   **Greetings**
第一课   问好

PART ONE   **Dialogue I: Exchanging Greetings**

I. Listening Comprehension (INTERPRETIVE)

A. Textbook Dialogue (Multiple Choice)

( ) **1.** What did the man say first to the woman?

    a. What's your name?
    b. I'm Mr. Wang.
    c. Are you Miss Li?
    d. How do you do!

( ) **2.** What is the woman's full name?

    a. Wang Peng
    b. Li You
    c. Xing Li
    d. Jiao Li You

( ) **3.** What is the man's full name?

    a. Wang Peng
    b. Li You
    c. Xing Wang
    d. Jiao Wang Peng

B. Workbook Dialogue I (Multiple Choice)

( ) **1.** These two people are _____.

    a. saying good-bye to each other
    b. asking each other's name
    c. greeting each other
    d. asking each other's nationality

C. Workbook Dialogue II (Multiple Choice)

(   ) **1.**   The two speakers are most likely _____.

    a.   brother and sister

    b.   father and daughter

    c.   two old friends being reunited

    d.   strangers getting acquainted

(   ) **2.**   Who are these two people? They are _____.

    a.   Mr. Li and Miss You

    b.   Mr. Li and Miss Li

    c.   Mr. Wang and Miss You

    d.   Mr. Wang and Miss Li

II. Speaking Exercises

A. Answer the questions in Chinese based on the Textbook Dialogue. (INTERPRETIVE AND PRESENTATIONAL)

1.   How does Mr. Wang greet Miss Li?

2.   What is Miss Li's reply?

3.   How does Mr. Wang ask what Miss Li's surname is?

4.   What is Mr. Wang's given name?

5.   How does Mr. Wang ask what Miss Li's given name is?

6.   What is Miss Li's given name?

B. You and your partner will participate in a simulated conversation. You will play two people who are meeting for the first time. Try to complete the following tasks in Chinese. (INTERPERSONAL)

1.   Exchange greetings with each other;

2.   Ask each other's last name and first name.

III. Reading Comprehension (INTERPRETIVE)

Read the passages below and answer the questions. (True/False)

A. 你好，先生。请问你贵姓？

(   ) **1.**   The question is addressed to a man.

(   ) **2.**   The speaker is talking to his/her friend.

( )**3.**   The sentence occurs at the end of a conversation.

( )**4.**   We do not know the addressee's family name.

B. 小姐，你好。我姓李，叫李朋。你呢？

( )**1.**   The speaker is talking to a man.

( )**2.**   We don't know whether the speaker is a man or a woman.

( )**3.**   We know the speaker's full name.

( )**4.**   The speaker knows the addressee's full name.

IV. Writing and Grammar Exercises (PRESENTATIONAL)

A. Rearrange the following words into a complete sentence. Use the English in parentheses as a clue.

1. 叫 / 名字 / 你 / 请问 / 什么

(May I ask what your name is?)

_____

B. Rewrite and answer the following questions in characters.

1.   Nǐ guì xìng?

_____   _____

2.   Nǐ jiào shénme míngzi?

_____   _____

C. Translate the following exchange into Chinese.

A: May I ask what your surname is?   _____

B: My surname is Li. My name is Li You.   _____

D. Write your Chinese name, if you have one, in characters.   _____

PART TWO Dialogue II: Asking about Someone's Nationality

 ## I. Listening Comprehension (INTERPRETIVE)

A. Textbook Dialogue (True/ False)

Quote the key sentence from the dialogue, in either *pinyin* or characters, to support your answer.

( ) **1.** Miss Li is a student.

_____

( ) **2.** Mr. Wang is a teacher.

_____

( ) **3.** Mr. Wang is American.

_____

( ) **4.** Miss Li is Chinese.

_____

B. Workbook Dialogue I (Multiple Choice)

( ) Which of the following is true?

    a. Both the man and the woman are Chinese.
    b. Both the man and the woman are American.
    c. The man is Chinese and the woman is American.
    d. The man is American and the woman is Chinese.

C. Workbook Dialogue II (Multiple Choice)

( ) Which of the following is true?

    a. Both the man and the woman are teachers.
    b. Both the man and the woman are students.
    c. The man is a teacher. The woman is a student.
    d. The man is a student. The woman is a teacher.

II. Speaking Exercises

A. Answer the following questions in Chinese based on the Textbook Dialogue. (PRESENTATIONAL)

1. How does Miss Li ask whether Mr. Wang is a teacher or not?
2. Is Mr. Wang a teacher?
3. Is Miss Li a teacher?
4. What is Mr. Wang's nationality?
5. What is Miss Li's nationality?

B. You meet a Chinese person on campus. Try to ask politely in Chinese whether he/she is a teacher. (Interpersonal)

C. You just met a foreign student who can speak Chinese. (INTERPERSONAL)

1. Ask him/her whether he/she is Chinese.
2. Tell him/her that you are American.

D. Introduce yourself in Chinese to your class. Tell your classmates what your Chinese name is and whether you are a student. (PRESENTATIONAL)

III. Reading Comprehension (INTERPRETIVE)

A. Match the sentences on the left column with the appropriate responses on the right column. Write down the letter in the parentheses.

( ) 1. 你好！　　　　　　　**A.** 是，我是老师。

( ) 2. 您贵姓？　　　　　　**B.** 不，我是中国人。

( ) 3. 你是美国人吗？　　　**C.** 我也是学生。

( ) 4. 你是老师吗？　　　　**D.** 我姓李。

( ) 5. 我是学生，你呢？　　**E.** 你好！

B. After reading the following passage, fill in the chart and answer the questions below.

王先生叫王师中。王师中是纽约人，不是中国人。王师中是学生，不是老师。李小姐是北京人，叫李美生。李美生是老师，不是学生。

	Gender	Given name	Nationality	Occupation	Hometown
王先生					
李小姐					

Questions (Multiple-choice):

( ) **1.** If you were the man's close friend, you would most often address him
   as _____.
   a. Wang Xiansheng   **b.** Xiansheng Wang
   c. Wang   **d.** Shizhong

( ) **2.** If you were introduced to the woman for the first time, it would be most
   appropriate for you to address her as _____.
   a. Li Xiaojie   **b.** Xiaojie Li
   c. Li Meisheng   **d.** Meisheng

C. Read the dialogue and answer the questions in English.

李先生：请问，你是王老师吗？

王小姐：是，我是。你是…

李先生：王老师，你好。我姓李，叫李大中。

王小姐：李大中，李大中… ò，李老师，是你 yà …你好，你好。

Questions:

1. Is this a dialogue between a teacher and a student?

_____

2. Are the two speakers very familiar with each other?

_____

3. What kind of tone of voice does the interjection "ò" bring to the dialogue?

_____

4. What kind of tone of voice does the particle "yà" bring to the dialogue?

_____

D. Reading Chinese Business Cards

1. Below are three Chinese business cards. Underline the characters denoting family names.

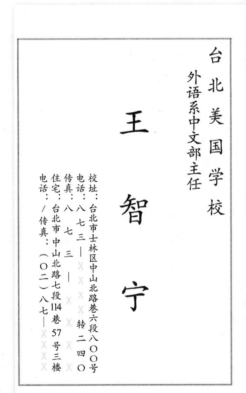

台北美国学校
外语系中文部主任

王 智 宁

校址：台北市士林区中山北路巷六段八〇〇号
电话：八七三—XXXX 转二四〇
传真：八七三—XXXX
住宅：台北市中山北路七段114巷57号三楼
电话：／传真：（〇二）八七—XXXX

中 外 合 资

常州华润装饰工程有限公司

CHANGZHOU HUA RUN DECORATION ENGINEERING CO. LTD

王 德 中
WANG   DE   ZHONG
董事 副总经理

地址：中国常州劳动中路４２号
ADD: NO42 LAO DONG RD(M) CHANGZHOU
电话 TEL: 8824743 881XXXX
传真 FAX: 0519–882XXXX
电挂 CABLE: 5000 邮编 P.C:213001
宅电 HOME:662XXXX

美国夏威夷大学东亚语文系教授

李 英 哲
YINGCHE LI

EAST ASIAN LANGUAGES AND LITERATURES
UNIVERSITY OF HAWAII
HONOLULU, HAWAII 96822
U.S.A

TEL: (808) 956-XXXX (0)
FAX: (808) 956-XXXX
INTERNET: yli@ssctang.hawaii.edu

2. Take a look at the following two Chinese business cards, and answer the questions in English.

美 国 在 合 协 会 华 语 学 校

王　俊　仁

台北市阳明山山仔后　　　　　　电话:(02) 2861- XXXX
爱富三街长生巷5号　　　　　　传真:(02) 2861- XXXX

外语教学与研究出版社
北京外语音像出版社

王　伟
音像中心

地址：北京市西三环北路 19 号 (北京外国语大学)
电话：(010)6891 XXXX
手机：13671 XXXX　　　　　　邮编：100089

1. What are their family names? _____

2. Which business card's owner works in Beijing, the one on the top or the bottom?

_____

IV. Writing and Grammar Exercises

A. Rewrite the following sentences in characters.

1. Qǐng wèn, nǐ shì xuésheng ma?

_____

2. Wǒ shì Zhōngguó rén. Nǐ ne?

_____

3. Wǒ bú xìng Wáng, wǒ xìng Lǐ.

_____

4. Nǐ shì lǎoshī, wǒ shì xuésheng.

_____

5. Nǐ shì Měiguó rén, wǒ yě shì Měiguó rén.

_____

B. Rearrange the following words into sentences, using the English in parentheses as clues. (PRESENTA-TIONAL)

1. 姓 / 王 / 吗 / 你
(Is your surname Wang?)

_____

2. 吗 / 是 / 你 / 学生 / 中国
(Are you a Chinese student?)

_____

3. 北京 / 是 / 人 / 我 / 不
(I am not from Beijing.)

_____

4. 小姐 / 先生 / 纽约人 / 纽约人 / 王 / 李 / 也 / 是 / 是
(Miss Wang is a New Yorker. Mr. Li is also from New York.)

_____

C. Answer the following questions in Chinese according to your own circumstances. (INTERPER-SONAL)

1. **A:** 你是学生吗？

B: _____

2. **A:** 你是北京人吗？

   B: _____

3. **A:** 李小姐是美国人。你呢？

   B: _____

4. **A:** 王先生是中国学生。你呢？

   B: _____

D. What's the Question? Write out the questions to which the following statements are the appropriate answers. (INTERPERSONAL)

EXAMPLE: 我是学生。 → <u>你是学生吗？</u>

1. 我是美国人。 → _____

2. 我姓李。 → _____

3. 王老师是北京人。 → _____

4. 李小姐不是老师。 → _____

5. 我也是学生。 → _____

E. Connect the following clauses into compound sentences using 也.

EXAMPLE: 李友是学生。/王朋是学生。→ <u>李友是学生，王朋也是学生。</u>

1. 你是美国人。/我是美国人。

_____

2. 李小姐不是中国人。/李先生不是中国人。

_____

3. 你不姓王。/我不姓王。

_____

4. 王先生不是纽约人。/李小姐不是纽约人。

_____

F. Complete the following conversation in characters based on the information given. The conversation has to be coherent. (INTERPERSONAL)

A: _____ 。   **B:** _____ 。

A: _____ , _____ ?   **B:** 我姓王。

A: _____ ?   **B:** 我叫王京。

A: _____ , _____ ?   **B:** 不，我不是，我是中国人。

A: _____ , _____ ?   **B:** 我也是。

G. Translate the following exchanges using the Chinese words or phrases learned in this lesson. (PRESENTATIONAL)

1. **A:** Is Mr. Wang Chinese?

    _____

    B: Yes, Mr. Wang is from Beijing.

    _____

2. **A:** Li You is a student. How about you?

    _____

    B: I am also a student.

    _____

3. **A:** I am from New York. Are you from New York, too?

    _____

    B: No, I am from Beijing.

    _____

4.   **A:** My family name is Wang. Is your family name Wang also?

_____

   B: No, my family name is not Wang. My family name is Li.

_____

H. Get ready to introduce yourself in Chinese by filling in the blanks below. (PRESENTATIONAL)

你好！我姓_____，我叫_____。我是_____人，

不是_____人。我是_____，不是_____。

LESSON 2 **Family**
第二课 家庭

PART ONE Dialogue I: Looking at a Family Photo

 ### I. Listening Comprehension (INTERPRETIVE)

A. Textbook Dialogue (True/False)

( ) **1.** Wang Peng knows the people in the picture.

( ) **2.** Gao doesn't have any older sisters.

( ) **3.** Gao's parents are in the picture.

( ) **4.** Gao's younger brother is also in the picture.

( ) **5.** Gao's older brother does not have any daughters.

B. Workbook Dialogue I (Multiple Choice)

( ) Who are the people in the picture?

    a. The woman's mother and younger sister.
    b. The woman's mother and older sister.
    c. The woman's older sister and younger sister.
    d. The woman's mother and her mother's sister.

C. Workbook Dialogue II (Multiple Choice)

( ) Which of the following statements is true?

    a. Wang Jing is the woman's sister.
    b. Wang Jing is the man's daughter.
    c. Wang Jing is not related to Mr. Wang.
    d. Wang Jing is not related to the woman.

II. Speaking Exercises

A. Answer the questions in Chinese based on the Textbook Dialogue. (INTERPRETIVE AND PRESENTATIONAL)

1. Whose photo is on the wall?

2. Who is the young lady in the picture?

3. Who is the boy in the picture?

4. Does Little Gao's big brother have a son or a daughter?

B. Introduce your parents to your classmates, using a family picture. Then ask your partner if he or she has any older sisters or younger brothers. (INTERPERSONAL)

III. Reading Comprehension

A. Match the following Chinese words with their English equivalents. (INTERPRETIVE)

( ) **1.** 爸爸   **A.** mother

( ) **2.** 大哥   **B.** boy

( ) **3.** 弟弟   **C.** older sister

( ) **4.** 女儿   **D.** eldest brother

( ) **5.** 妈妈   **E.** younger brother

( ) **6.** 姐姐   **F.** son

( ) **7.** 儿子   **G.** girl

( ) **8.** 男孩子   **H.** father

( ) **9.** 女孩子   **I.** daughter

B. Match the questions on the left with the appropriate replies on the right. (INTERPRETIVE AND INTERPERSONAL)

( ) **1.** 这个人是谁？   **A.** 我没有弟弟。

( ) **2.** 这是你的照片吗？   **B.** 这是我爸爸。

( ) **3.** 这个男孩子是你弟弟吗？   **C.** 他有儿子，没有女儿

( ) **4.** 你妹妹是学生吗？   **D.** 不是，他是王老师的儿子

( ) **5.** 李先生有女儿吗？   **E.** 是我的。

( ) **6.** 你有弟弟吗？   **F.** 她是学生。

C. Read the following dialogue and answer the questions. (True/False) (INTERPRETIVE)

王朋：李友，这个女孩子是你吗？

李友：不，她是我妈妈。

王朋：你妈妈？这个男孩子是你爸爸吗？

李友：不是，他是我妈妈的大哥。

Questions:

( ) **1.** What are the speakers doing while talking?

    a. Looking at Wang Peng's picture.
    b. Looking at a picture taken many years ago.
    c. Looking at a picture they took yesterday.
    d. Looking at Li You's parents' picture.

( ) **2.** The picture features _____.

    a. Wang Peng and Li You
    b. Li You and her mother
    c. Wang Peng and Li You's mother
    d. Li You's mother and Li You's uncle

IV. Writing and Grammar Exercises

A. Fill in the blanks with 这 or 那 based on the descriptions for each situation.

1. You point to a person standing about thirty feet away, and say:

    ＿＿＿＿个人是我的老师，他是北京人。

2. You are holding a family photo in your hand, and say:

    ＿＿＿＿是我爸爸，＿＿＿＿是我妈妈。

3. You look down the hallway and recognize someone, and say:

    ＿＿＿＿个人叫李生，是李友的爸爸。

4. You introduce to your friend a girl sitting at the same table, and say:

    ＿＿＿＿是李先生的女儿，李小约。

B. Look at the picture and answer the following questions. (INTERPERSONAL)

1. 这个人是谁？/他是谁？＿＿＿＿＿＿＿＿＿＿

2. 他是中国人吗？/这个人是中国人吗？

    ＿＿＿＿＿＿＿＿＿＿＿＿＿＿＿＿＿＿＿＿

C. Answer the following questions in Chinese according to your own circumstances. (INTERPERSONAL)

1. 你有姐姐吗？

    ＿＿＿＿＿＿＿＿＿＿＿＿＿＿＿＿＿＿＿＿

2. 你有弟弟吗？

    ＿＿＿＿＿＿＿＿＿＿＿＿＿＿＿＿＿＿＿＿

3. 你爸爸叫什么名字？

_____

4. 你妈妈是老师吗？

_____

D. What's the Question? Focus on the underlined words, and write out the questions to which the following statements are the appropriate answers. (INTERPERSONAL)

EXAMPLE: <u>他</u>是王朋。 → 谁是王朋？

1. 小李有<u>两</u>个姐姐。

_____

2. 这是<u>王老师</u>的照片。

_____

3. 那个男孩子是<u>王朋</u>。

_____

E. Translate the following exchanges into Chinese. (PRESENTATIONAL)

1. A: Little Wang, is this your photograph?

_____

B: This is not my photograph.

_____

2. A: Mr. Wang has no sons. How about Mr. Li?

_____

B: He doesn't, either.

_____

3. **A:**   Who is this young lady?

   _____

   B: She's my older sister.

   _____

4. **A:**   Does your big brother have a son?

   _____

   B: No, he doesn't have any sons, nor does he have any daughters.

   _____

F. Go online and look up information about the Brady Bunch. Based on the information gathered, write down how many sons and daughters Mr. and Mrs. Brady have, and what the children's names are. It would be even better if you could include a photo of the Bradys and introduce them one by one to your teacher. (PRESENTATIONAL)

PART TWO   Dialogue II: Asking about Someone's Family

 I. Listening Comprehension (INTERPRETIVE)

A. Textbook Dialogue (Multiple Choice)

( ) **1.** How many people are there in Bai Ying'ai's family?

     a. 3   **b.** 4   **c.** 5   **d.** 6

( ) **2.** How many people are there in Li You's family?

     a. 3   **b.** 4   **c.** 5   **d.** 6

( ) **3.** How many younger sisters does Bai Ying'ai have?

     a. 0   **b.** 1   **c.** 2   **d.** 3

( ) **4.** How many older sisters does Li You have?

     a. 0   **b.** 1   **c.** 2   **d.** 3

( ) **5.** How many older brothers does Bai Ying'ai have?

     a. 0   **b.** 1   **c.** 2   **d.** 3

( ) **6.** How many younger brothers does Bai Ying'ai have?

     a. 0   **b.** 1   **c.** 2   **d.** 3

( ) **7.** How many children do Bai Ying'ai's parents have?

     a. 2   **b.** 3   **c.** 4   **d.** 5

( ) **8.** How many sons do Li You's parents have?

     a. 0   **b.** 1   **c.** 2   **d.** 3

( ) **9.** Bai Ying'ai's father is a _____.

     a. lawyer   **b.** teacher   **c.** doctor   **d.** student

( ) **10.** Li You's mother is a _____.

     a. lawyer   **b.** teacher   **c.** doctor   **d.** student

B. Workbook Dialogue I (Multiple Choice)

( ) **1.** Which of the following is true?

    a. Both the man and the woman have older brothers.
    b. Both the man and the woman have younger brothers.
    c. The man has an older brother but no younger brothers.
    d. The man has a younger brother but no older brothers.

( ) **2.** Why does the woman laugh at the end of the conversation? Because she finds it funny that _____.

    a. neither the man nor she herself has any younger brothers
    b. neither the man nor she herself has any older brothers
    c. the man failed to count himself as his older brother's younger brother
    d. the man failed to count himself as his younger brother's older brother

C. Workbook Dialogue II (Multiple Choice)

( ) **1.** The man's mother is a _____.

    a. teacher
    b. student
    c. doctor
    d. lawyer

( ) **2.** The woman's father is a _____.

    a. teacher
    b. student
    c. doctor
    d. lawyer

D. Workbook Dialogue III (Multiple Choice)

( ) **1.** How many brothers does the woman have?

    a. 1   **b.** 2   **c.** 3   **d.** 4

( ) **2.** How many daughters do the woman's parents have?

    a. 1   **b.** 2   **c.** 3   **d.** 4

( ) **3.** How many people in the woman's family are older than herself?

    a. 2   **b.** 3   **c.** 4   **d.** 5

( ) **4.** How many people in the man's family are younger than himself?

    a. 0   **b.** 1   **c.** 2   **d.** 3

( ) **5.** Why do the speakers disagree on the number of the people in the man's family? Because he forgot to include _____.

    a. his older brother   **b.** his younger sister

    c. his younger brother   **d.** himself

II. Speaking Exercises

A. Answer the questions in Chinese based on the Textbook Dialogue. (INTERPRETIVE AND PRESENTATIONAL)

1. How many people are there in Bai Ying'ai's family?
2. How many brothers and sisters does Li You have?
3. What is Bai Ying'ai's father's occupation?
4. What are Bai Ying'ai's mother's and Li You's mother's occupations?
5. How many people are there in Li You's family?

B. Find or draw a family picture and use it to introduce your family members to your class. (PRESENTATIONAL)

C. Show your family picture to your partner and ask questions about each other's pictures, such as who each person is, whether your partner has any brothers or sisters, and what each of his/her family members does. (INTERPERSONAL)

III. Reading Comprehension (INTERPRETIVE)

A. Mr. Wang and Mr. Li are neighbors. Let's get to know their families. Read the following passage and answer the questions below.

王先生是学生。他爸爸是律师，妈妈是英文老师。王先生的哥哥是医生。李先生和她妹妹都是学生。李先生的爸爸和姐姐都是医生，妈妈是老师。

Questions:

1. If the two families vacation together, how many airplane tickets should they book?

    _____

2. How many doctors are there between the two families? Who are they?

    _____

3. If Mr. Wang's mother has a colleague in the Li family, who is most likely to be that person?

_____

4. How many students are there between the two families?

_____

5. What does Mr. Li's father do? Is anyone from the Wang family in the same profession?

_____

B. Read the dialogue below:

小王：请问，你爸爸是律师吗？

小高：不，他是老师。我家有两个老师，两个医生，一个律师。

小王：你家有五口人吗？

小高：不，我家有四口人。我和我妈妈都是医生。我哥哥是老师，也是

律师。

Check the proper spaces in the following form to indicate the profession of each member of Little Gao's family:

	Little Gao	Father	Mother	Older Brother
Lawyer				
Doctor				
Teacher				

Questions (True/False):

(   ) **1.**   Little Wang seems to know Little Gao's family very well.

(   ) **2.**   Little Gao seems to have miscounted the people in his family.

(   ) **3.**   Little Gao's older brother is not only a teacher, but also a lawyer.

C. Look at the following business card, and answer the questions. (True/False)

韩 沐 新   律师   合伙人

世联新纪元律师事务所

地址: 北京建国门外大街 xxxx   邮编: 100004
电话: (8610)6515 xxxx   直线: (8610)6515 xxxx
手机: 139011 xxxx   传真: (8610)6528 xxxx
E-mail: muxinh@c-li xxxx   网址: //www.c-li xxxx

( )**1.**   This person's family name is Li.
( )**2.**   This person is a doctor.
( )**3.**   This person does business in Beijing.

IV. Writing and Grammar Exercises

A. Answer the following questions about your siblings in complete sentences, using 有 or 没有.
If the answer is affirmative, state how many siblings you have. (INTERPERSONAL)

EXAMPLES: **A:** 你有哥哥吗？   **B:** 我没有哥哥。

           B: 你有哥哥吗？   **A:** 我有两个哥哥。

1. A: 你有哥哥吗？   **B:** _____ 。

2. A: 你有姐姐吗？   **B:** _____ 。

3. A: 你有弟弟吗？   **B:** _____ 。

4. A: 你有妹妹吗？   **B:** _____ 。

B. Rewrite the following sentences using 都.

EXAMPLES: 小高是学生，王朋也是学生。 → 小高和王朋都是学生。

1. 高文中有姐姐，李友也有姐姐。

_____ 。

2. 那个男孩子姓李，那个女孩子也姓李。

_____。

3. 李友没有我的照片，王朋也没有我的照片。

_____。

4. 她哥哥不是律师，她弟弟也不是律师。

_____。

5. 这个人不叫白英爱，那个人也不叫白英爱。

_____。

C. Fill in the blanks with the appropriate question words. (什么、谁、谁的、几)

1. **A:** 他妹妹叫_____名字？   **B:** 他妹妹叫高美美。

2. **A:** 李老师家有_____口人？   **B:** 他家有三口人。

3. **A:** 他爸爸做_____工作？   **B:** 他爸爸是医生。

4. **A:** 那个美国人是_____？   **B:** 他叫David Smith，是我的老师。

5. **A:** 那是_____照片？   **B:** 那是白律师的照片。

D. Translate the following exchanges into Chinese. (PRESENTATIONAL)

1. **A:** How many people are there in Mr. Wang's family?

_____

   B: There are five people in his family.

_____

2. **A:** What do his parents do?

_____

   B: Both his mother and father are teachers.

_____

3. A: How many daughters does he have?

_____

B: None. He has three boys.

_____

4. A: My dad is a doctor. My mom is a lawyer. How about your mom and dad?

_____

B: My mom is a lawyer, too. My dad is a teacher.

_____

5. A and **B** are looking at a picture on B's desk. Translate their conversation into Chinese.

A: Who is this?

_____

B: This is my older sister. Her name is Wang Xiaoying.

_____

A: What does she do?

_____

B: My sister and I both are college students...How many sisters do you have?

_____

A: I have an older sister, too. Here is a picture of her. She has a daughter.

_____

E. Write about your family: (PRESENTATIONAL)

1. List your family members in Chinese.

2. To the best of your Chinese ability, tell what each of your family members does. It's okay to write their occupations in *pinyin*.

3. Draft an oral presentation: Write a brief introduction of your family using the framework provided. Memorize the introduction, bring in a family picture of yours, and give your presentation in class.

你好，我姓＿＿＿＿＿，我叫＿＿＿＿＿＿＿＿。我是＿＿＿＿＿学生。

我家有＿＿＿＿＿口人，＿＿＿＿＿＿＿＿＿＿和我。这是我家人的照

片。这是我爸爸，这是我妈妈，这个人是我＿＿＿＿＿＿＿…。

我爸爸是＿＿＿＿＿＿＿，妈妈是＿＿＿＿＿＿。＿＿＿＿＿＿＿

是…。

LESSON 3   # Dates and Time
第三课   时间

PART ONE   ## Dialogue I: Taking Someone Out to Eat on His/Her Birthday

I. Listening Comprehension (INTERPRETIVE)

A. Textbook Dialogue (True/False)

( ) **1.**   Gao Wenzhong is eighteen years old this year.

( ) **2.**   September 12 is Thursday.

( ) **3.**   Bai Ying'ai will treat Gao Wenzhong to a dinner on Thursday.

( ) **4.**   Gao Wenzhong is American, but he likes Chinese food.

( ) **5.**   Bai Ying'ai refuses to eat Chinese food.

( ) **6.**   They will have dinner together at 6:30 p.m.

B. Workbook Dialogue I (Multiple Choice)

( ) **1.**   Today's date is _____.

    a. May 10   **b.** June 10   **c.** October 5   **d.** October 6

( ) **2.**   What day is today?

    a. Thursday   **b.** Friday   **c.** Saturday   **d.** Sunday

( ) **3.**   What day is October 7? It is _____.

    a. Thursday   **b.** Friday   **c.** Saturday   **d.** Sunday

C. Workbook Dialogue II (Multiple Choice)

( ) **1.**   What time does the man propose to meet for the appointment?

    a. 6:30   **b.** 7:00   **c.** 7:30   **d.** 8:00

(   ) **2.**   What time do they finally agree upon?

    a.   6:30   **b.**   7:00   **c.**   7:30   **d.**   8:00

(   ) **3.**   What day are they going to meet?

    a.   Thursday   **b.**   Friday   **c.**   Saturday   **d.**   Sunday

II. Speaking Exercises

A. Answer the questions in Chinese based on the Textbook Dialogue. (INTERPRETIVE AND PRESENTATIONAL)

1.   When is Gao Wenzhong's birthday?
2.   How old is Gao Wenzhong?
3.   Who is going to treat whom?
4.   What is Gao Wenzhong's nationality?
5.   What kind of food are they going to have?
6.   What time is the dinner?

B. With a partner, participate in a simulated conversation. Today is your partner's birthday. Find out how old he/she is and offer to take him/her out to dinner. Ask him/her if he/she prefers Chinese or American food and decide the time for the dinner. (INTERPERSONAL)

III. Reading Comprehension (INTERPRETIVE)

A. Read the calendar and answer the questions. (Multiple Choice)

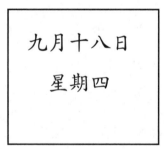

Questions:

(   ) **1.**   What day of the week was September 15?

    a.   Monday

    b.   Tuesday

    c.   Friday

    d.   Sunday

( ) **2.** What is the date of next Thursday?

    a. September 22

    b. September 23

    c. September 24

    d. September 25

B. Fill in the blanks in English based on the calendar.

1. The date on this calendar is _____.

2. The day of the week is _____.

3. Next month is _____.

4. The day after tomorrow is a _____.

C. Which of the following is the correct way to say "June 3, 2009" in Chinese?

1. 6月3号2009年

2. 3号6月2009年

3. 6月2009年3号

4. 2009年6月3号

The correct answer is: _____

D. Read the passage below and answer the questions. (True/False)

这个星期六是十一月二号，是小王的妈妈的生日。小王请他妈妈吃饭。王妈妈很喜欢我，小王也请我吃饭。吃什么呢？王妈妈是北京人，喜欢吃中国菜。我是纽约人，可是我也喜欢吃中国菜。

Questions:

( ) **1.** Saturday is Little Wang's birthday.

( ) **2.** Little Wang's mother will take her son to dinner this Saturday.

( ) **3.** The speaker seems to know Little Wang's mother well.

( ) **4.** The speaker is American, and Little Wang's mother is Chinese.

( ) **5.** Most likely they will have a Chinese dinner on Saturday.

E. This is a flier for a museum exhibition. What were the dates for the exhibition, and on which university campus was it held?

吉金铸国史

周原出土铜器精粹展

时间：五月四日至八月三十日　AM9:00–PM4:30
展出地点：纽英大学考古与艺术博物馆

IV. Writing and Grammar Exercises

A. Write the following numbers in Chinese characters. (PRESENTATIONAL)

1. 15 → _____

2. 93 → _____

3. 47 → _____

4. 62 → _____

5. Your phone number → _____

6. Your birthday → _____月_____号

B. Write out the questions to which the following statements are the appropriate answers. Use 还是 in each question. (INTERPERSONAL)

EXAMPLE: **A:** 王朋  （<u>王朋是中国人还是美国人？</u>）

B: 王朋是中国人。

1. **A:** 你 _____?

B: 我喜欢吃美国菜。

2. **A:** 李友的爸爸 _____?

B: 他是律师。

3. **A:** 高文中 _____?

B: 高文中有姐姐。

C. Rearrange the following Chinese words into sentences, using the English sentences as clues. (PRESENTATIONAL)

1. 我 / 晚饭 / 你 / 怎么样 / 吃 / 请 / 星期四
   (I'll take you out to dinner on Thursday. How's that?)

   _____

2. 星期四 / 星期五 / 晚饭 / 我 / 你 / 还是 / 请 / 吃
   (Are you taking me out to dinner on Thursday or Friday?)

   _____

3. 哥哥 / 小白 / 喜欢 / 他 / 我 / 我 / 可是 / 不 / 喜欢
   (I do not like Little Bai, but I like his older brother.)

   _____

4. 美国人 / 美国菜 / 可是 / 他 / 不 / 喜欢 / 吃 / 是
   (He is American, but he does not like eating American food.)

   _____

D. Answer the following questions according to your own circumstances. (INTERPERSONAL)

1. **A:** 你今年多大？

   B: _____

2. **A:** 你的生日（是）几月几号？

   B: _____

3. **A:** 你喜欢吃美国菜还是中国菜？

   B: _____

E. Translate the following exchanges into Chinese. (PRESENTATIONAL)

1. **A:** When is your birthday?

   _____

   B: My birthday is September 30.

   _____

2. **A:** What day of the week is September 30?

   _____

   B: September 30 is Friday.

   _____

3. **A:** How old are you?

   _____

   B: I am eighteen.

   _____

4. **A:** How about I treat you to dinner on Thursday?

   _____

   B: Great! Thanks. See you Thursday.

   _____

5. Little Wang's girlfriend has never met Little Wang's parents. She is planning a dinner date and wants to invite Little Wang's parents. She wants to find out more information about her guests...Translate their conversation using Chinese characters.

Little Wang: What time are we having dinner on Saturday night?

   _____

Girlfriend: How about 7:30?

   _____

Little Wang: Okay. Whom are we inviting for dinner?

   _____

Girlfriend: We'll invite your mom and dad.

   _____

Little Wang: Great.

_____

Girlfriend: Do they like American or Chinese food?

_____

Little Wang: They like American, and they like Chinese, too.

_____

F. Complete the following tasks in Chinese. (PRESENTATIONAL)

   1. Write down today's date in Chinese.

   _____

   2. Write down the current time in Chinese.

   _____

   3. Who's your idol/hero? Your idol/hero could be one of your family members or someone famous. If your idol/hero is someone famous, then go online and find out his/her age, birthday, family members, and what cuisine he/she prefers. Write a personal profile on your idol/hero in Chinese, and share it with your teacher/class.

PART TWO — Dialogue II: Inviting Someone to Dinner

I. Listening Comprehension

A. Textbook Dialogue (True/False)

( ) **1.**   Wang Peng is not busy today.

( ) **2.**   Wang Peng will be busy tomorrow.

( ) **3.**   Bai Ying'ai is inviting Wang Peng to dinner.

( ) **4.**   Tomorrow is Bai Ying'ai's birthday.

( ) **5.**   Li You is Bai Ying'ai's schoolmate.

B. Workbook Dialogue I (True/False)

( ) **1.**   Both speakers in the dialogue are Chinese.

( ) **2.**   The man invites the woman to dinner because it will be his birthday tomorrow.

( ) **3.**   The man likes Chinese food.

( ) **4.**   The woman likes only American food.

C. Workbook Dialogue II (True/False)

( ) **1.**   Today the woman is busy.

( ) **2.**   Today the man is not busy.

( ) **3.**   Tomorrow both the man and the woman will be busy.

II. Speaking Exercises

A. Answer the questions in Chinese based on the Textbook Dialogue. (INTERPRETIVE AND PRESENTATIONAL)

1.   Why does Bai Ying'ai ask if Wang Peng is busy or not tomorrow?

2.   When is Wang Peng busy?

3.   Who else will go to the dinner tomorrow?

4.   Does Bai Ying'ai know Li You? How do you know?

B. Ask your partner today's date, the day of the week, and the current time. (INTERPERSONAL)

C. Find out your partner's age and birthday, and set up a dinner appointment to celebrate his/her birthday. (INTERPERSONAL)

D. With a partner, participate in a simulated conversation. Your partner would like to take you out to dinner tomorrow, but you will be busy. Suggest another day for the dinner and decide on a time. (INTERPERSONAL)

III. Reading Comprehension (INTERPRETIVE)

A. Rewrite the following times in ordinary numeral notation (e.g., 1:00, 2:15, 3:30 p.m.).

1. 三点：_____

2. 六点三刻：_____

3. 晚上八点：_____

4. 晚上九点一刻：_____

5. 晚上十一点半：_____

B. Read the dialogue and answer the questions. (True/False)

男：你好。我想请你吃晚饭，怎么样？

女：是吗？我不认识你，你为什么请我吃饭？

男：因为今天是我的生日，可是没有人请我吃饭，所以…

女：先生，你为什么不请你的朋友吃饭？

男：因为他们今天都很忙。

Questions:

( ) **1.**   The two people are friends.
( ) **2.**   The man needs someone to celebrate his birthday with him.
( ) **3.**   The woman accepts the man's invitation readily.
( ) **4.**   The woman is the only one that the man invites to dinner.
( ) **5.**   According to the man, his friends are too busy today to celebrate his birthday.

C. Read the following dialogue and answer the questions. (Multiple Choice)

小白：今天是几月几号？

小李：今天是二月二十八号。

小白：是吗？明天是我的生日。我的生日是二月二十九号。明天
        晚上我请你吃晚饭，怎么样？

小李：太好了，谢谢。可是明天不是二月二十九号。

小白：那明天是几月几号？

小李：明天是三月一号。你今年没有生日。

Questions:

( ) **1.** Which of the following statements is true?

   a. Little Bai has been expecting her birthday all week.
   b. Little Bai almost failed to realize that her birthday was approaching.
   c. Little Li has been expecting Little Bai's birthday.

( ) **2.** Tomorrow will be _____.

   a. February 28
   b. February 29
   c. March 1

( ) **3.** Which of the following statements is true?

   a. Little Bai has forgotten her birthday.
   b. Little Li gave the wrong date for tomorrow.
   c. Little Bai's birthday is off this year's calendar.

D. Like people in other cultures, the Chinese often have to fill out forms with personal information. Let's see whether we can complete part of such a form.

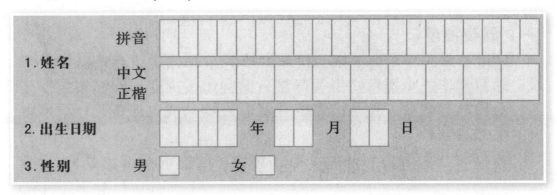

IV. Writing and Grammar Exercises

A. Rewrite the following dates or time phrases in Chinese characters.
(PRESENTATIONAL)

1. November 12 → _____

2. Friday evening → _____

3. 7:00 this evening → _____

4. 8:30 p.m. Saturday → _____

5. quarter after nine → _____

B. Complete the following exchanges. (INTERPERSONAL)

1. **A:** 今天（是）几月几号？   **B:** _____ 。

2. **A:** 你的生日（是）_____？ **B:** 我的生日（是）_____。

3. **A:** 你今年多大？   **B:** _____ 。

4. **A:** 现在几点？   **B:** 现在_____ 。

5. **A:** _____ ？   **B:** 我五点三刻吃晚饭。

C. What's the Question? Write out the questions using "A-not-A" form. (INTERPERSONAL)

EXAMPLE: **A:** <u>王先生是不是北京人</u>？   **B:** 王先生是北京人。

1. **A:** _____ ？

   B: 小李没有弟弟。

2. **A:** _____ ？

   B: 小王不喜欢吃美国菜。

3. **A:** _____ ？

   B: 小高的姐姐工作。

4. A: _____ ?

    B: 高律师明天很忙。

D. Based on the Dialogue, answer the following questions with 因为 . (INTERPERSONAL)

1. 白英爱为什么请高文中吃饭？

_____

2. 白英爱为什么问(to ask)王朋忙不忙？

_____

3. 王朋为什么认识李友？

_____

E. Rewrite the following sentences using 还.

EXAMPLE: 我有一个哥哥。我有一个弟弟。

    → <u>我有一个哥哥，还有一个弟弟。</u>

1. 她喜欢吃中国菜。她喜欢吃美国菜。

_____

2. 他认识王朋。他认识李友。

_____

3. 白英爱有她哥哥的照片。白英爱有她妹妹的照片。

_____

F. Translate the following exchanges into Chinese. (PRESENTATIONAL)

1. **A:** What time is it right now?

    _____

    B: It's 8:45.

    _____

2. **A:** Are you busy or not this evening?

    _____

    B: I have things to do this evening. I am available tomorrow evening.

    _____

3. **A:** Does your brother have a girlfriend or not?

    _____

    B: He doesn't.

    _____

    A: Great! I'd like to invite him to dinner on Friday.

    _____

    B: He's busy on Friday, but I am free.

    _____

    A: Really? But I like your brother, not you.

    _____

G. Write a birthday party invitation card in Chinese. Make sure to include the date, the day of the week, and the time. Don't forget to indicate what kind of food you will serve. The location is at your house.

我家

H. Write a note to your friend inviting him/her to have dinner with you tomorrow because tomorrow is your birthday.

LESSON 4   Hobbies

第四课　爱好

PART ONE   Dialogue I: Talking about Hobbies

I. Listening Comprehension (INTERPRETIVE)

A. Textbook Dialogue (True/False)

( ) **1.**   Gao Wenzhong likes music.

( ) **2.**   Bai Ying'ai reads a lot every weekend.

( ) **3.**   Bai Ying'ai likes to sing and dance on weekends.

( ) **4.**   Both Gao Wenzhong and Bai Ying'ai seem to like to go to the movies.

( ) **5.**   Gao Wenzhong is inviting Bai Ying'ai to dinner and a film tonight.

( ) **6.**   Gao Wenzhong and Bai Ying'ai will be joined by two friends.

B. Workbook Dialogue I (Multiple Choice)

( ) **1.**   What does the man like to do the most?

a. Listen to music	**b.** Play ball
c. Go to the movies	**d.** Go dancing

( ) **2.**   If the man and the woman decide to do something together, they will most likely go to _____.

a. a movie	**b.** a concert
c. a dance	**d.** a ball game

C. Workbook Dialogue II (Multiple Choice)

( ) **1.**   The man invites the woman to _____.

a. a dinner	**b.** a movie
c. a dance	**d.** a concert

( ) **2.** The man invites the woman because _____.

    a. she has invited him to a dinner before

    b. she likes watching movies

    c. tomorrow is his birthday

    d. he has too much free time

( ) **3.** Which of the following statements is true?

    a. The woman doesn't accept the invitation although she will not be busy tomorrow.

    b. The woman doesn't accept the invitation because she'll be busy tomorrow.

    c. The woman accepts the invitation although she'll be busy tomorrow.

    d. The woman accepts the invitation because she will not be busy tomorrow.

II. Speaking Exercises

A. Answer the questions in Chinese based on the Textbook Dialogue. (INTERPRETIVE AND PRESENTATIONAL)

    1. What does Gao Wenzhong like to do on weekends?

    2. What does Bai Ying'ai like to do on weekends?

    3. What will Bai Ying'ai and Gao Wenzhong do this evening?

    4. Who is treating this evening?

    5. Who else may also go this evening?

B. Discuss your interests and hobbies with your friends, and then set up a date with them based on your common interests. (INTERPERSONAL)

III. Reading Comprehension (INTERPRETIVE)

A. Draw a line connecting each phrase with the activity it represents.

1. 打球

2. 跳舞

3. 唱歌

4. 听音乐

5. 看电视

B. Read the paragraph, and pencil in Little Gao's activities in English on the day planner. Note the activities, the times of the activities, and the people who are doing the activities.

　　这个星期小高天天晚上都很忙。今天星期一，晚上八点小高请朋友跳舞，明天晚上六点半请同学吃饭，星期三晚上九点一刻请女朋友看电影，星期四晚上打球，星期五晚上唱歌。那周末他做什么呢？看书吗？不对！小高不喜欢看书，周末那两天他看电视、看电视、看电视…

Monday	Tuesday	Wednesday	Thursday	Friday	Saturday	Sunday

C. Read the passage and answer the following questions in English:

　　我大哥认识一个女孩子，她的名字叫李明英。李小姐今年二十岁，是大学生。我大哥很喜欢她，常常请她吃晚饭。周末两个人喜欢去跳舞、看电影。可是李小姐的爸爸和妈妈不喜欢我大哥，因为他今年三十八岁，可是没有工作。我也不喜欢他们两个人做男女朋友，因为李小姐是我的同学。

1. What are the three things that we know about Miss Li?

　　_____

2. What do the two lovebirds like to do on weekends?

　　_____

3. What are the two reasons that Miss Li's parents don't like their daughter dating the narrator's big brother?

　　_____

4. What's the narrator's attitude toward the relationship? Why does she feel this way?

　　_____

D. This is a heading clipped from a Chinese newspaper. What listings does it refer to? What were the dates the listings were good for?

_____

IV. Writing and Grammar Exercises

A. Give a written report on what these four people like or don't like to do. (PRESENTATIONAL)

	✗				✓	✓
	✓					✗
	✓		✓	✗		
		✓				✗

1.  _____

2.  _____

3.  _____

4. _____

B. Use a word or phrase from each of the four following groups to make four sentences based on the Chinese word order: Subject + Time + Verb + Object. (INTERPRETIVE AND PRESENTATIONAL)

> 美国菜，球，音乐，电影
>
> 明天晚上，这个周末，星期四，今天
>
> 去看，去听，去打，去吃
>
> 我们，我爸爸妈妈，小白和小高，王朋和李友

1. _____ 。

2. _____ 。

3. _____ 。

4. _____ 。

C. Translate the following exchanges into Chinese using the words and phrases in parentheses. (PRESENTATIONAL)

1. **A:** Do you go to see movies often on weekends?

   _____

   B: I am busy on weekends. I work.

   _____

2. **A:** How about I take you dancing tonight?

   _____

   B: Thanks. But I don't like dancing.

   _____

3. A: What do you like to do?

_____

B: Sometimes I like reading, and sometimes I also like listening to music.

_____

4. A: Why is it your treat today?

_____

B: Because it was your treat yesterday. It's my treat today.

_____

5. A: You like watching foreign films, right?

_____

B: That's correct. I watch foreign films often.

_____

D. Continue to work on your self-introduction. (INTERPRETIVE AND PRESENTATIONAL)

我姓_____，我叫_____。我是_____学生。我家有

_____口人，_____和我。我爸爸是_____，

妈妈是_____。

我喜欢_____，有的时候也喜欢_____，

可是我不喜欢_____。我周末_____忙，常常_____

_____。

Dialogue II: Would You Like to Play Ball?

PART TWO

💿 I. Listening Comprehension (INTERPRETIVE)

A. Textbook Dialogue (True/False)

( ) **1.** Gao Wenzhong does not like playing ball.

( ) **2.** Wang Peng wants to play ball this weekend.

( ) **3.** Gao Wenzhong is very interested in watching a ball game.

( ) **4.** Wang Peng is going out to eat with Gao Wenzhong.

( ) **5.** Gao Wenzhong likes to sleep.

( ) **6.** In the end, Wang Peng gives up the idea of going out with Gao Wenzhong.

B. Workbook Dialogue I (True/False)

( ) **1.** The woman doesn't like Chinese movies because her Chinese is not good enough.

( ) **2.** The woman prefers American movies over Chinese movies.

( ) **3.** The man agrees that American movies are more interesting.

C. Workbook Dialogue II (True/False)

( ) **1.** The woman invites the man to a concert.

( ) **2.** The man wants to play ball.

( ) **3.** The man invites the woman to go dancing.

D. Workbook Narrative (Multiple Choice)

( ) **1.** The speaker probably spends most of his spare time _____.

    a. in movie theaters

    b. in concert halls

    c. in front of a TV set

    d. in a library

( ) **2.** According to the speaker, Wang Peng loves _____.

    a. movies and TV

    b. to dance and read

    c. dancing and music

    d. books only

( ) **3.** Which of the following statements is true about the speaker and Wang Peng?

    a. Wang Peng likes to read.

    b. The speaker likes to watch TV.

    c. Both the speaker and Wang Peng like to dance.

    d. Wang Peng and the speaker are classmates.

II. Speaking Exercises

A. Answer the following questions in Chinese based on the Textbook Dialogue. (INTERPRETIVE AND PRESENTATIONAL)

    1. How does Wang Peng greet Gao Wenzhong?

    2. Does Gao Wenzhong want to play ball? Why?

    3. Does Gao Wenzhong want to go to the movies? Why?

    4. What does Gao Wenzhong like to do?

    5. What did Wang Peng finally decide to do this weekend?

B. With a partner, participate in a simulated conversation. Your partner is inviting you to do something. Keep rejecting his/her suggestions and give reasons why you do not like those activities. (INTERPERSONAL)

III. Reading Comprehension

A. Match the questions on the left with the appropriate replies on the right. (INTERPRETIVE AND INTERPERSONAL)

( ) **1.** 你叫什么名字？   **A.** 我明天不忙。

( ) **2.** 这是你弟弟吗？   **B.** 今天晚上我很忙。

( ) **3.** 你明天忙不忙？   **C.** 我想看一个外国电影。

( ) **4.** 你认识小高吗？   **D.** 不，这是我哥哥。

( ) **5.** 你喜欢听音乐吗？   **E.** 因为我喜欢吃美国菜。

( ) **6.** 为什么你请我看电影？   **F.** 认识，他是我同学。

( ) **7.** 为什么我们不吃中国菜？   **G.** 我叫王朋。

( ) **8.** 我们去打球，好吗？   **H.** 我觉得听音乐没有意思。

( ) **9.** 这个周末你做什么？   **I.** 我不想打球。

( ) **10.** 今天晚上我去找你，好吗？ **J.** 因为今天是你的生日。

B. Read the passage and answer the questions. (Multiple Choice) (INTERPRETIVE)

小王和小李是同学。小王是英国人，他喜欢打球、看电视和看书。小李是美国人，她喜欢听音乐、唱歌和跳舞。他们都喜欢看电影，可是小王只喜欢看美国电影，小李觉得美国电影没有意思，她只喜欢看外国电影。她觉得中国电影很有意思。

Questions:

( ) **1.** What activities does Little Wang enjoy?

    a. Watching TV and listening to music
    b. Watching Chinese movies and dancing
    c. Watching American movies and singing
    d. Playing ball and reading

( ) **2.** What does Little Li like to do?

    a. Watch TV and listen to music
    b. Watch Chinese movies and dance
    c. Watch American movies and dance
    d. Play ball and read

( ) **3.** Which of the following statements is true?

    a. Little Wang and Little Li both like to watch TV.
    b. Little Wang is American and he likes American movies.
    c. Little Li is Chinese but she likes American movies.
    d. Little Wang and Little Li go to the same school.

( ) **4.** If Little Wang and Little Li want to do something they are both interested in, where can they go together?

    a. To a ball game.
    b. To a library.
    c. To a dance party.
    d. None of the above.

C. Read the following dialogue and answer the questions. (True/False) (INTERPRETIVE)

小王：你喜欢看美国电影还是外国电影？

老李：我不喜欢看美国电影，也不喜欢看外国电影。

小王：你觉得中国音乐有意思还是美国音乐有意思？

老李：我觉得中国音乐和美国音乐都没有意思。

小王：你常常看中文书还是英文书？

老李：我不看中文书，也不看英文书。

小王：那你喜欢吃中国菜还是美国菜？

老李：中国菜和美国菜我都喜欢吃。

Questions:

( ) **1.** This conversation most likely takes place in the United States.

( ) **2.** Old Li does not like American movies, but likes European ones.

( ) **3.** Old Li feels that both Chinese music and American music are boring.

( ) **4.** When Old Li reads, the book must be in a language other than English or Chinese.

( ) **5.** It seems Old Li does not like anything American or Chinese.

D. Read the following passage and answer the questions in English. (INTERPRETIVE)

小李很喜欢打球，可是他的女朋友小文觉得打球没有意思，她只喜欢看电影。明天是星期六，也是小文的生日。小李和小文想去看电影。可是看什么电影呢？小李觉得 "The Benchwarmers" 这个电影有很多人打球，很有意思。小文不喜欢打球，可是也想去看那个电影。小李和小文都很高兴，他们明天下午三点半去看电影。

Questions:

1. What does Little Li like to do?

_____

2. Why does Little Li want to see a movie with Little Wen tomorrow?

_____

3. What makes the movie "The Benchwarmers" special to Little Li?

_____

4. Why are Little Li and Little Wen both happy?

_____

E. Listed below are the TV channels on a Chinese television network. Locate the channels for movies and music respectively.

今明电视节目安排

8月1日 周一电视

第一电视台-1(综合频道)

19:55 电视剧:冼星海(5、6)
21:40 纪实十分

第二电视台-2(经济频道)

20:25 经济与法
21:30 经济半小时

第三电视台-3(综艺频道)

18:30 综艺快报
19:05 动物世界
21:15 快乐驿站

第四电视台-4(国际频道)

20:10 走遍中国
20:40 海峡两岸
21:00 中国新闻
21:30 今日关注
22:00 中国文艺

第五电视台-5(体育频道)

18:55 巅峰时刻
21:30 体育世界

第六电视台-6(电影频道)

21:48 世界电影之旅之资讯快车

第八电视台-8(电视剧频道)

19:30 电视剧:国家机密(15—17)

第十电视台-10(科教频道)

20:10 历程
20:30 走近科学
21:40 讲述

第十二电视台-12(社会与法频道)

20:00 大家看法
23:10 心理访谈
23:30 电视剧:公安局长(7、8)

第十三电视台-新闻频道

20:30 新闻会客厅
21:30 国际观察
21:55 天气资讯

第十四电视台-少儿频道

19:00 中国动画(精品版)
19:30 智慧树
20:00 动漫世界

第十五电视台-音乐频道

20:10 经典

IV. Writing and Grammar Exercises

A. Rearrange the following Chinese words into sentences, using the English sentences as clues. (PRESENTATIONAL)

1. 觉得 / 这个 / 没有 / 电影 / 有 / 意思 / 你

   (Do you think this movie is interesting?)

   _____

2. 王朋 / 去 / 周末 / 和 / 李友 / 这个 / 打球

   (Wang Peng and Li You will go play ball this weekend.)

   _____

3. 今天晚上 / 他 / 看 / 电视 / 想 / 不 / 听 / 音乐 / 想

   (Tonight he wants to watch TV, not listen to music.)

   _____

B. Based on the Dialogue, answer the following questions using 因为 . . . 所以 . . . (INTERPRE-TIVE AND INTERPERSONAL)

1. **A:** 高文中为什么请白英爱看电影？

   B: _____

2. **A:** 高文中为什么不想去打球？

   B: _____

3. **A:** 高文中为什么不想去看球？

   B: _____

C. Answer the following questions according to your own circumstances. (INTERPERSONAL)

1. **A:** 你周末常常做什么？

   B: _____ 。

2. **A:** 你喜欢看美国电影还是外国电影？

   B: _____ 。

3. A: 你今天晚上想几点睡觉？

B: _____ 。

4. A: 你觉得打球有意思还是跳舞有意思？

B: _____ 。

D. Translate the following exchanges into Chinese. (PRESENTATIONAL)

1. A: Little Wang, long time no see. Have you been busy?

_____

B: Long time no see, Little Gao. I've been busy. How about you?

_____

A: I am busy, too.

_____

2. A: Let's go dancing this weekend, okay?

_____

B: I don't want to go. I only want to get some sleep.

_____

3. A: I'd like to take you to see a foreign film.

_____

B: Thank you. But I think foreign films are boring.

_____

A: Never mind. I'll go find someone else.

_____

4. A: What would you like to do tonight? How about watching TV?

_____

B: I think watching TV is boring. I like singing and dancing. I'd like to go singing tonight.

_____

A: OK.

_____

5. **A:**   Today is my birthday. I am 19 years old. My friends will take me out for dinner and

   dancing tonight.

   _____

   B: You like dancing, correct?

   _____

   A: Right, I like dancing. I often dance on weekends. How about you?

   _____

   B: I think dancing is boring.

   _____

   A: Is that so?!

   _____

E. The following chart shows what Little Wang wishes to do this coming week. Write a report based on the information given. (PRESENTATIONAL)

	Monday	Tuesday	Wednesday	Thursday	Friday	Saturday	Sunday
Little Wang							

LESSON 5   Visiting Friends
第五课   看朋友

PART ONE   Dialogue: Visiting a Friend's Home

I. Listening Comprehension (INTERPRETIVE)

A. Textbook Dialogue (True/False)

( ) **1.** Wang Peng and Li You had met Gao Wenzhong's older sister before.

( ) **2.** Li You was very happy to meet Gao Wenzhong's sister.

( ) **3.** Gao Wenzhong's sister is a student.

( ) **4.** Li You likes to drink tea.

( ) **5.** Gao Wenzhong's sister gave Li You a cola.

B. Workbook Dialogue I (True/False)

( ) **1.** The man and the woman are speaking on the phone.

( ) **2.** The man and the woman have never met each other before.

( ) **3.** The man is looking for his younger brother.

C. Workbook Dialogue II (Multiple Choice)

( ) **1.** The dialogue most likely takes place between

    a. two strangers.
    b. parent and child.
    c. two friends.
    d. a teacher and a student.

( ) **2.** Which of the following statements about the woman is true?

    a. She doesn't like TV in general but she likes what is on TV tonight.
    b. She doesn't like TV in general and she likes what is on TV tonight even less.
    c. She likes TV in general but she doesn't like what is on TV tonight.
    d. She likes TV in general and she particularly likes what is on TV tonight.

( ) **3.** What will they most likely end up doing?

    a. Watching TV

    b. Seeing a Chinese movie

    c. Reading an American novel

    d. Listening to Chinese music

D. Workbook Dialogue III (Multiple Choice)

( ) **1.** Which of the following is the correct order of the woman's preferences?

    a. Coffee, tea

    b. Cola, coffee

    c. Coffee, cola

    d. Tea, coffee

( ) **2.** Which beverage does the man not have?

    a. Tea

    b. Water

    c. Cola

    d. Coffee

( ) **3.** Which beverage does the woman finally get?

    a. Tea

    b. Water

    c. Cola

    d. Coffee

II. Speaking Exercises

A. Answer the questions in Chinese based on the Textbook Dialogue. (INTERPRETIVE AND PRESENTATIONAL)

1. Who went to Gao Wenzhong's house?

2. Had Wang Peng and Li You met Gao Wenzhong's sister before?

3. What is Gao Wenzhong's older sister's name?

4. How is Gao Wenzhong's house?

5. Where does Gao Wenzhong's older sister work?

6. What did Wang Peng want to drink?

7. Why did Li You ask for a glass of water?

B. With a partner, participate in a simulated conversation. You are talking to a person whom you are meeting for the first time. Exchange basic greetings, ask each other's name, and find out if he/she is a student, where he/she works, and what his/her hobbies are. (INTERPERSONAL)

C. With a partner, participate in a simulated conversation. You are visiting a friend's home. Compliment your friend on his/her house. Your friend offers you something to drink, but you just want a glass of water. (INTERPERSONAL)

III. Reading Comprehension (INTERPRETIVE)

A. Read the following description carefully and match each of the names with the proper beverage by placing the letters in the appropriate parentheses.

小高、小白和小王都是同学。小高不喜欢喝咖啡，也不喜欢喝茶。小白不喝可乐，也不常喝咖啡。小王只喜欢喝咖啡。

( ) **1.** Little Gao   **a.** tea

( ) **2.** Little Bai   **b.** coffee

( ) **3.** Little Wang   **c.** cola

B. Read the dialogue and answer the questions. (True/False)

（王中去他的同学李文家玩儿。）

李文：王中，你想喝点儿什么？

王中：给我一瓶可乐吧。

李文：对不起，我家没有可乐。

王中：那给我一杯茶，好吗？

李文：对不起，也没有茶。

王中：那我喝一杯咖啡吧。

李文：对不起，我只有水。

王中：你家很大，也很漂亮，可是…

Questions:

( ) **1.**   Wang Zhong is visiting Li Wen's home.

( ) **2.**   Wang Zhong seems to like tea better than water.

( ) **3.**   Li Wen's refrigerator is full of all kinds of beverages.

( ) **4.**   Wang Zhong is impressed by the beverages that Li Wen has offered.

C. This is a beverage menu. You have 90 Taiwanese dollars in your pocket and need to order three different beverages. What can you order?

饮料

可乐/雪碧/健怡可乐 ……	M$25 L$30
柳橙汁 ……	M$35
鲜榨柳橙汁 ……	M$50
摩斯矿泉水 ……	$18
冰咖啡/冰红茶 ……	M$30 L$35
热咖啡/热红茶 ……	$30
奇异蔬果汁 ……	$50
可可亚(季节限定) ……	$30
咖啡欧蕾(季节限定) ……	$30

1. _____   2. _____   3. _____

IV. Writing and Grammar Exercises

A. Look at the visual clues below and write in Chinese characters using appropriate numbers, measure words, and nouns. (PRESENTATIONAL)

1.

2.

3.

_____   _____   _____

B. Rearrange the following Chinese words into sentences, using the English sentences as clues. (PRESENTATIONAL)

1. 常常 / 王老师 / 在图书馆 / 看书
   (Professor Wang often reads at the library.)

   _____

2. 看电视 / 周末 / 我的同学 / 在家
   (My classmate watches TV at home on weekends.)

   _____

3. 小白 / 工作 / 星期五 / 在哪儿
   (Where does Little Bai work on Fridays?)

   _____

C. Answer the following questions according to your own circumstances. (INTERPERSONAL)

1. 你的老师高不高？

   _____

2. 你的医生好不好？

   _____

3. 你的英文书有没有意思？

   _____

4. 你今天高兴不高兴？

   _____

5. 你们的学校漂亮吗？

   _____

6. 你们的图书馆大吗？

   _____

D. Little Li is a waiter at a restaurant. Mr. Gao, a customer, walks into the restaurant. The following is part of the conversation between Little Li and Mr. Gao. Complete the conversation by filling in the blanks with the right letters representing the phrases or sentences provided. Each letter can only be used once. (INTERPERSONAL)

> **a** 您要英国茶还是中国茶 **b** 可以，可以 **c** 好久不见
>
> **d** 请坐，请坐 **e** 高先生 **f** 请进，请进 **g** 您想喝点什么

Little Li: _____ , _____ 。 Mr. Gao: 小李，好久不见。

Little Li: _____ 。 Mr. Gao: 好，谢谢。

Little Li: _____ 。 Mr. Gao: 我不想坐这儿，我想坐

那儿。可以吗？

Little Li: _____ 。

Little Li: _____ ？ Mr. Gao: 我想喝茶。

Little Li: _____ ？ Mr. Gao: 给我一杯英国茶吧！

E. Translate the following exchanges into Chinese. (PRESENTATIONAL)

1. **A:** Let me introduce... This is my classmate, Li Ming.

   _____

   B: Mr. Li, my name is Wang Ying. Glad to meet you.

   _____

   C: Miss Wang, very glad to meet you, too.

   _____

2. **A:** Where do you work?

   _____

   B: I work at a school.

   _____

3. A: What would you like to do this weekend? See a movie or go dancing?

_____

   B: Let's go dancing!

_____

4. A: Would you like to have something to drink? Coffee or tea?

_____

   B: Give me a cup of coffee then.

_____

F. Suppose you are running an etiquette school, and you are teaching your students how to be a nice host and a good guest. List some must-learn sentences below as part of your training manual, so your students know what to say to their hosts or guests when they are in China. (PRESENTATIONAL)

Nice Host

1. _____

2. _____

3. _____

4. _____

5. _____

...

Good Guest

1. _____

2. _____

3. _____

4. _____

5. _____

...

PART TWO Narrative: At a Friend's House

I. Listening Comprehension (INTERPRETIVE)

A. Textbook Narrative (True/False)

( ) **1.** Gao Wenzhong's older sister works in a library.

( ) **2.** Wang Peng had two glasses of water at the Gaos' place.

( ) **3.** Li You did not drink tea at the Gaos' place.

( ) **4.** Wang Peng and Li You chatted and watched TV at the Gaos'.

( ) **5.** Wang Peng and Li You left the Gaos' house at noon.

B. Workbook Narrative (True/False)

( ) **1.** The speaker thinks that Little Bai and Little Li are old friends.

( ) **2.** The three people are most likely at the speaker's place.

( ) **3.** Little Bai told Little Li that he works in the library.

C. Workbook Dialogue (Multiple Choice)

( ) **1.** Where were Little Bai and his younger brother Saturday night? They were
_____.

    a. at home

    b. at Little Gao's place

    c. at Little Li's place

    d. at Little Bai's brother's place

( ) **2.** What did Little Bai's brother do at the party? He was _____.

    a. having tea

    b. watching TV

    c. chatting

    d. dancing

( ) **3.** Little Bai spent most of the evening _____.

    a. drinking and watching TV

    b. chatting and watching TV

    c. having tea and chatting

    d. drinking, chatting and watching TV

II. Speaking Exercises

A. Answer the questions in Chinese based on the Textbook Narrative. (INTERPRETIVE AND PRESENTATIONAL)

   1.   Why did Wang Peng and Li You go to Gao Wenzhong's house?

   2.   Where does Wenzhong's sister work?

   3.   What did Wang Peng drink? How much?

   4.   What did Wang Peng and Li You do at Wenzhong's house?

   5.   When did Wang Peng and Li You go home?

B. With a partner, participate in a simulated conversation. Ask each other what you drank last night, how much, and what else you did last night. Then report in a narrative to your teacher/class based on the information gathered. (INTERPERSONAL AND PRESENTATIONAL)

III. Reading Comprehension (INTERPRETIVE)

A. Read the following note, and answer the questions in English.

小张：

　　明天晚上七点半学校有一个中国电影，我们一起去看，好吗？我明天晚上来找你。

小高

十月五日晚上九点半

   1.   Who wrote the note?

   _____

   2.   What time is the movie?

   _____

   3.   Where is the movie?

   _____

   4.   What date is the movie?

   _____

   5.   When was the note written?

   _____

B. Read the passage and answer the questions.

　　昨天是小李的生日，小李请了小高、小张和王朋三个同学去她家吃饭。他们七点吃晚饭。小李的家不大，可是很漂亮。小李的爸爸是老师，他很有意思。小李的妈妈是医生，昨天很忙，九点才回家吃晚饭。小李的哥哥和姐姐都不在家吃饭。王朋和小李的爸爸妈妈一起喝茶、聊天。小高、小张和小李一起喝可乐、看电视。小高、小张和王朋十一点才回家。

Questions: (True/False)

( ) **1.** Little Li's home is both large and beautiful.
( ) **2.** Little Li celebrated her birthday with her classmates but not with her entire family.
( ) **3.** Wang Peng drank cola with his friends.
( ) **4.** Little Li's friends left her home about the same time.

Questions: (Multiple Choice)

( ) **5.** Who was late for dinner last night?

　　a. Little Gao
　　b. Little Zhang
　　c. Little Li's father
　　d. Little Li's mother

( ) **6.** Which of the following statements is true?

　　a. Little Li's mother is a teacher.
　　b. Little Li's father is an interesting person.
　　c. Little Li's brother and sister were home last night.
　　d. Wang Peng talked with Little Li all evening.

C. Read the passage and answer the questions. (True/False)

　　今天小高去找他的同学小王，小王的妹妹也在家。可是小高不认识小王的妹妹。小王介绍了一下。小王的妹妹也是他们学校的学生。她很漂亮，喜欢唱歌和看书。这个周末小高想请小王的妹妹去喝咖啡、看电影。

Questions:

( ) **1.**   Little Gao has met Little Wang's sister before.

( ) **2.**   Little Gao and Little Wang's sister attend the same school.

( ) **3.**   Little Gao's sister likes to dance.

( ) **4.**   Little Gao would like to invite Little Wang and his sister to see a movie this weekend.

IV. Writing and Grammar Exercises

A. The following chart shows what Little Gao did and didn't do last night. Write the questions and the answers based on the chart. (INTERPERSONAL)

	Example	1.	2.	3.	4.	5.
	X	✓	X	✓	X	X

EXAMPLE **A:** 他昨天晚上打球了吗？ → **B:** 他昨天晚上没打球。

1. A: _____ ? 　　**B:** _____ 。

2. A: _____ ? 　　**B:** _____ 。

3. A: _____ ? 　　**B:** _____ 。

4. A: _____ ? 　　**B:** _____ 。

5. A: _____ ? 　　**B:** _____ 。

B. Little Wang went to a party last night. The visuals below show what he drank and how much he drank at the party. Ask and answer questions based on the graphics. (INTERPERSONAL)

EXAMPLE: 1. 2. 3.

EXAMPLE: **A:** 他喝咖啡了吗？ **B:** 他喝咖啡了。

A: 他喝了几杯咖啡？ **B:** 他喝了两杯咖啡。

1. **A:** _____? **B:** _____。
   A: _____? **B:** _____。
2. **A:** _____? **B:** _____。
   A: _____? **B:** _____。
3. **A:** _____? **B:** _____。
   A: _____? **B:** _____。

C. Little Li is always late, but she doesn't realize it. Now you are going to summarize what her friends have told you and make her realize that she is a repeat offender.

EXAMPLE:　　6:00pm　请她吃晚饭　6:30pm

→ 我们六点请她吃晚饭，她六点半才来。

1. 7:30pm　看电影　7:45pm

→ _____

2. 8:00am　工作　8:15am

→ _____

3. 6:30pm　打球　7:00pm

→ _____

D. Translate the following sentences into Chinese. (PRESENTATIONAL)

1. A: Did you play ball last night?

_____

B: No, I didn't. I was too busy.

_____

2. A: Did you have coffee?

_____

B: I didn't. I only drank two glasses of water.

_____

3. A: Why didn't you go to bed until 12:00 a.m.?

_____

B: Because I saw two movies, and didn't go home until 11:30 p.m.

_____

4. I met Miss Li at school. She is tall and pretty. She likes to chat. We often chat and have tea together. She thinks dancing is fun. I will take her dancing tonight.

_____

_____

_____

_____

E. Describe a recent visit to your friend's house. Make sure that you mention what you did and what you drank.

Let's Review (LESSONS 1–5)

I. How do we say these words?

Write down their correct pronunciation and tones in *pinyin*.

1. 你们＿＿＿＿＿＿＿＿＿＿＿   你好＿＿＿＿＿＿＿＿＿＿＿

2. 不错＿＿＿＿＿＿＿＿＿＿＿   不来＿＿＿＿＿＿＿＿＿＿＿

3. 音乐＿＿＿＿＿＿＿＿＿＿＿   可乐＿＿＿＿＿＿＿＿＿＿＿

4. 觉得＿＿＿＿＿＿＿＿＿＿＿   睡觉＿＿＿＿＿＿＿＿＿＿＿

II. Group the characters according to their radicals.

> 喝 馆 孩 打 晚 星 绍 快
> 说 找 今 时 国 他 图 睡 吃 杯 学 妹 呢
> 们 忙 谁 姓 看 给 样 饭 回

Radicals   **Characters**

1. ＿＿＿＿＿   ＿＿＿＿＿＿＿＿＿＿＿＿＿＿＿＿＿＿＿＿＿

2. ＿＿＿＿＿   ＿＿＿＿＿＿＿＿＿＿＿＿＿＿＿＿＿＿＿＿＿

3. ＿＿＿＿＿   ＿＿＿＿＿＿＿＿＿＿＿＿＿＿＿＿＿＿＿＿＿

4. _____ _____

5. _____ _____

6. _____ _____

7. _____ _____

8. _____ _____

9. _____ _____

10. _____ _____

11. _____ _____

12. _____ _____

13. _____ _____

III. Which of the following verbs are VO compounds?

吃饭   跳舞   工作   认识   请客

IV. Getting to Know You (INTERPERSONAL AND PRESENTATIONAL)

Put your Chinese to use. Interview your classmates to find out their likes and habits. After a brief Q & A session, jot down and organize the information you have gathered, and then present an oral or written report to introduce your classmates to others.

Here is a sample questionnaire to get you started. Of course, you can replace these questions with your own, and add more if you think it's appropriate.

1. Personal and Family Background

你今年多大？ _____

你的生日（是）几月几号？ _____

你是纽约人吗？ _____

你家有几口人？有没有兄(xiōng, elder brother)弟姐妹？ _____

_____

你爸爸、妈妈做什么工作？他们在哪儿工作？ _____

_____

2. Likes and Dislikes

你喜欢做什么？打球还是看电影？ _____

_____

你觉得做什么很有意思/没有意思？ _____

_____

你喜欢听音乐吗？ _____

你喜欢听谁的音乐？ _____

你喜欢跳舞吗？ _____

你喜欢跳什么舞？ _____

你喜欢喝什么？水、茶、可乐还是咖啡？ _____

_____

3. Habits and Routines

你常常看电视吗？ _____

你常常在哪儿看书？ _____

你常常晚上几点睡觉？ _____

你周末常常做什么？ _____

LESSON 6 Making Appointments
第六课　约时间

PART ONE **Dialogue I: Calling One's Teacher**

I. Listening Comprehension (INTERPRETIVE)

A. Textbook Dialogue (Multiple Choice)

( ) **1.** Why is Li You calling Teacher Chang?

   a. Li You cannot come to school because she is sick.
   b. Li You wants to ask some questions.
   c. Li You wants to know where Teacher Chang's office is.
   d. Li You wants to know where the meeting is.

( ) **2.** What is Teacher Chang going to do this afternoon?

   a. Teach two classes.
   b. Go home early.
   c. Attend a meeting.
   d. Go to a doctor's office.

( ) **3.** How many classes will Teacher Chang teach tomorrow morning?

   a. One.
   b. Two.
   c. Three.
   d. Four.

( ) **4.** What will Teacher Chang be doing at 3:30 tomorrow afternoon?

   a. Attending a meeting.
   b. Giving an exam.
   c. Working in her office.
   d. Seeing a doctor.

( ) **5.** Where is Li You going to meet Teacher Chang?

  a. In Teacher Chang's office.

  b. In the classroom.

  c. In the meeting room.

  d. In the library.

( ) **6.** When will Li You meet with Teacher Chang tomorrow?

  a. 9:00 a.m.

  b. 10:30 a.m.

  c. 3:00 p.m.

  d. 4:30 p.m.

B. Workbook Dialogue I (True/False)

( ) **1.** The woman in the dialogue is the caller's sister.

( ) **2.** The caller asks to speak to Little Gao.

( ) **3.** There is going to be a Chinese film tonight.

( ) **4.** The woman will most likely stay home tonight.

C. Workbook Dialogue II (Multiple Choice)

( ) **1.** Which of the following statements is true?

  a. The woman invites the man to a dinner party at her home.

  b. The woman invites the man to a dance at her home.

  c. The woman hopes to go to the dinner party at the man's home.

  d. The woman hopes to go to the dance at the man's home.

( ) **2.** Why can't the man go? Because

  a. he is giving a party.

  b. he has to prepare for a test.

  c. he is not allowed to go.

  d. he doesn't like the host.

II. Speaking Exercises

A. Answer the following questions in Chinese based on the Textbook Dialogue. (INTERPRETIVE AND PRESENTATIONAL)

  1. Why did Li You call Teacher Chang?

  2. Will Teacher Chang be free this afternoon? Why or why not?

  3. Will Teacher Chang be free tomorrow morning? Why or why not?

4. What will Teacher Chang do at three o'clock tomorrow afternoon?

5. When will Li You go to visit Teacher Chang?

B. Participate in a simulated conversation with your teacher. You would like to make an appointment with him/her. Your teacher happens to be busy at the time you suggest. Ask your teacher when he/she will be available. Decide on a time and place to meet. (INTERPERSONAL)

III. Reading Comprehension

A. Match the expressions on the left with the responses on the right. (INTERPRETIVE AND INTERPERSONAL)

( ) **1.** 你是哪位？   **A.** 认识你们我也很高兴。

( ) **2.** 我们今天晚上去   **B.** 不客气。

跳舞，好吗？

( ) **3.** 喝点儿茶，怎么样？   **C.** 再见。

( ) **4.** 喂，请问小白在吗？   **D.** 对不起，我不喜欢喝茶。

( ) **5.** 认识你很高兴。   **E.** 对不起，她去图书馆了。

( ) **6.** 谢谢。   **F.** 对不起，我今天下午要开会。

( ) **7.** 明天见。   **G.** 对不起，我明天要考试。

( ) **8.** 今天下午我来   **H.** 我是王朋。

找你，好吗？

B. Read Teacher Li's schedule below and answer the questions in English. (INTERPRETIVE)

小高的中文老师李老师很忙。我们一起看一下她星期三做什么。

8:30	到学校去上课	
9:00–10:00	上一年级中文课	
10:15–11:00	去图书馆找书	
12:00–1:00	在办公室吃饭	
1:30–2:30	上二年级中文课	
2:45–3:30	开会	
4:00–5:00	学生来他的办公室问问题	

1. 李老师星期三有几节课？

   _____

2. 李老师的学生星期三有没有考试？

   _____

3. 李老师回家吃午饭 (wǔfàn, lunch) 吗？

   _____

4. 李老师上了一年级中文课以后做什么？

   _____

5. 要是小高想去李老师的办公室问问题，什么时候去方便？

   _____

6. 你觉得李老师星期三几点钟才可以回家？

   _____

C. Read the following dialogue and answer the questions. (INTERPRETIVE)

（李友给王朋打电话。李友问了王朋几个问题。）

王朋：还有别的问题吗？

李友：我还有一个问题。

王朋：你问吧。

李友：你明天下午有空吗？我想找你聊天儿。

王朋：对不起，我明天下午要开会。

李友：明天晚上怎么样？

王朋：我明天晚上也没有时间。我想请一个女孩子去跳舞。

李友：… 那算了。

王朋：你也认识那个女孩子。

李友：是吗？她叫什么名字？

王朋：她姓李，叫李友。

Questions: (True/False)

(   ) **1.** Li You's schedule for tomorrow seems quite flexible.

(   ) **2.** Wang Peng hopes to see Li You tomorrow.

(   ) **3.** Li You does not know the girl that Wang Peng wants to take to the dance.

(Multiple Choice)

(   ) **4.** What will Wang Peng do tomorrow?

    a. He will have a meeting in the afternoon and chat with Li You in the evening.

    b. He will meet with Li You in the afternoon and go to a concert with another girl in the evening.

    c. He will have a meeting in the afternoon and go to a concert with Li You in the evening.

(   ) **5.** On hearing of Wang Peng's plan for tomorrow evening, Li You must be _____.

    a. first disappointed and then very happy

    b. first very happy and then disappointed

    c. neither happy nor disappointed

IV. Writing and Grammar Exercises

A. Look at the visuals given and write in Chinese characters using appropriate numbers, measure words, and nouns. (PRESENTATIONAL)

EXAMPLE:    →   两个问题

1. _____   2. _____   3. _____   4. _____

B. What would you like to do tomorrow if you had no classes, no exams, no meetings, etc.? Let's practice by using 要是 with the help of the words and the visuals given. (PRESENTATIONAL AND INTERPERSONAL)

EXAMPLE: 没课 →

→ **A.** <u>要是你明天没课，你做什么？</u> **B.** <u>我去图书馆看书</u>。

1. 没事儿 →

→ **A:** _____ ? **B:** _____ 。

2. 有空儿 →

→ **A:** _____ ? **B:** _____ 。

3. 不开会 →

→ **A:** _____ ? **B:** _____ 。

4. 不考试 →

→ **A:** _____ ? **B:** _____ 。

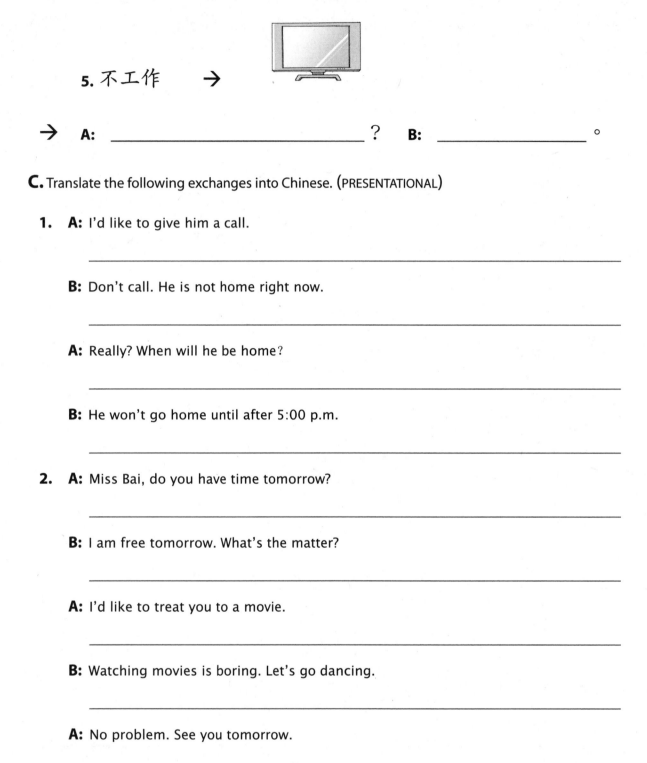

5. 不工作　　→

→　**A:** _____ ?　**B:** _____ 。

C. Translate the following exchanges into Chinese. (PRESENTATIONAL)

1. **A:** I'd like to give him a call.

    _____

    B: Don't call. He is not home right now.

    _____

    A: Really? When will he be home?

    _____

    B: He won't go home until after 5:00 p.m.

    _____

2. **A:** Miss Bai, do you have time tomorrow?

    _____

    B: I am free tomorrow. What's the matter?

    _____

    A: I'd like to treat you to a movie.

    _____

    B: Watching movies is boring. Let's go dancing.

    _____

    A: No problem. See you tomorrow.

    _____

3. **A:** Hello! Is Teacher Chang there?

_____

B: This is she. Who's this, please?

_____

A: Teacher Chang, how are you? This is Gao Wenzhong.

_____

B: Hi, Gao Wenzhong, is there anything that I can do for you?

_____

A: I'd like to go to your office right now to ask you a question. Is that okay?

_____

B: Sure. I'll wait for you in my office.

_____

A: Thanks.

_____

D. Ask your teacher what his/her typical school day is like. Take notes, and transcribe what he/she has told you. (PRESENTATIONAL AND INTERPRETIVE)

PART TWO   Dialogue II: Calling a Friend for Help

I. Listening Comprehension (INTERPRETIVE)

A. Textbook Dialogue (True/False)

( ) **1.** Li You is returning Wang Peng's phone call.

( ) **2.** Li You has an examination next week.

( ) **3.** Li You is asking Wang Peng to practice Chinese with her.

( ) **4.** Wang Peng is inviting Li You to have coffee.

( ) **5.** Wang Peng is going to have dinner with Li You this evening.

( ) **6.** Wang Peng does not know exactly when he is going to call Li You.

B. Workbook Dialogue I (True/False)

( ) **1.** Tomorrow will be Friday.

( ) **2.** Li You cannot go to the dinner tomorrow because she will be busy.

( ) **3.** Li You will be practicing Chinese this evening.

( ) **4.** Wang Peng promises to help Li You with her Chinese tomorrow at 6:30 p.m.

C. Workbook Dialogue II (True/False)

( ) **1.** Wang Peng cannot help Li You because he has classes tomorrow afternoon.

( ) **2.** Wang Peng asks Little Bai to help Li You with her Chinese.

( ) **3.** Little Bai and Li You will meet at 2 p.m. tomorrow in the library.

II. Speaking Exercises

A. Answer the questions in Chinese based on the Textbook Dialogue. (INTERPRETIVE AND PRESENTATIONAL)

1. Why did Li You call Wang Peng?

2. Why did Wang Peng ask Li You to invite him for coffee?

3. What will Wang Peng do tonight?

4. Will Wang Peng meet with Li You tonight?

5. What will Li You do tonight?

B. Work with a partner. You call your partner for a favor and promise a treat in return. You would like to meet him/her tonight, but he/she is going to see a movie. He/she promises that he/she will give you a call when he/she comes back. (INTERPERSONAL)

III. Reading Comprehension (INTERPRETIVE)

A. Below is a page of Little Gao's appointment book. Take a look at the things that he plans to do next week and answer the following questions in English.

1. 他什么时候考中文？

   _____

2. 他跟王朋在哪儿练习中文？

   _____

3. 他为什么星期五要打电话回家？

   _____

4. 他星期几没事儿？

   _____

5. 他星期四要做什么？

_____

6. 他星期天在哪儿吃饭？

_____

B. Read the following email passage and answer the questions. (True/False)

小白：

我下午在图书馆等你，可是你没来。我四点给你打了一个电话，可是你不在宿舍。我们什么时候可以见面？我明天晚上要跟小王一起去看电影，可是要是你明天晚上有空，我可以不去看电影。今天晚上我在家等你的电话。

小高

Questions:

( ) **1.** Little Bai and Little Gao were in the library this afternoon.

( ) **2.** Little Bai did not leave her dorm until 4:00 pm.

( ) **3.** Little Gao wants to see Little Bai.

( ) **4.** We do not know for sure what Little Gao will be doing tomorrow evening.

( ) **5.** Little Gao considers an appointment with Little Bai more important than seeing a movie with Little Wang.

( ) **6.** Little Gao will call Little Bai again this evening.

C. This is a note that Little Bai left for Wang Peng. Read the note and answer the questions in English.

王朋：

我知道你今天下午没有课，所以来找你，可是你不在宿舍。我昨天到常老师的办公室去，请他帮我练习说中文，可是他很忙。我今天上午给老师打电话，问他今天下午方便不方便，可是他明天下午两点以后才有空儿。我明天上午要考中文，你可以帮我准备一下吗？请你回来以后给我打电话。谢谢！

小白

五点半

Questions:

1. Where did Wang Peng find this note?

   _____

2. When was this note written?

   _____

3. Why didn't Little Bai call before dropping in?

   _____

4. Why did Little Bai look for Wang Peng?

   _____

5. Did Little Bai get help from her teacher? Explain the situation.

   _____

6. What do you think Wang Peng will do on seeing this note?

   _____

D. After reading the note above, Wang Peng found another note. Read it and answer the questions below.

王朋：

　　李友今天下午两点半给你打电话。她今天下午两点才知道星期五上午有中文考试，所以她今天晚上不跟你去跳舞。要是你有空，她想请你今天下午帮她练习中文，她考试以后请你看电影。你回来以后给她打电话吧。

小高

两点三刻

Questions (True/False)

( ) **1.**   This note was left by Li You.

( ) **2.**   Wang Peng was not in at 2:30 p.m. but was back by 2:45 p.m.

( ) **3.**   At 1:30 p.m. today Li You still planned to go to the dance.

( ) **4.**   We do not know when Wang Peng will call Li You back.

( ) **5.**   Li You was certain that Wang Peng would be available this afternoon.

(Multiple Choice)

( ) **6.**   Which of the statements is true?

  a.   Li You had been told last Friday that there would be an exam.

  b.   Li You was told this afternoon that there would be an exam on Friday.

  c.   Li You was told that yesterday evening's exam was postponed till Friday.

( ) **7.**   Li You hopes to take Wang Peng to a movie this _____.

  a.   Wednesday evening

  b.   Thursday evening

  c.   Friday evening

IV. Writing and Grammar Exercises

A. Following the example, make sentences using the given words, 得 and 别.

EXAMPLE: **A:** 我想去找同学聊天儿。（准备考试）

→   **B:** <u>别</u>去找同学聊天，你<u>得</u>准备考试。

1.   **A:** 我想看电视。   （看书）

    B: _____

2. **A:** 我想喝咖啡。 （睡觉）

   B: _____

3. **A:** 我想跟朋友玩儿。 （工作）

   B: _____

B. Answer the following questions according to your own circumstances. (PRESENTATIONAL)

1. 你常常给谁打电话？

   _____

2. 你是大学几年级的学生？

   _____

3. 你星期一有几节课？

   _____

4. 你星期四几点有中文课？

   _____

5. 你常常跟谁一起练习说中文？

   _____

C. Rearrange the following Chinese words into sentences, using the English sentences as clues. (PRESENTATIONAL)

1. 四点 / 我 / 办公室 / 电话 / 在 / 明天 / 等 / 以后 /
   下午 / 你的
   (I will be waiting for your phone call in the office after 4:00 p.m. tomorrow.)

   _____

2. 朋友 / 才 / 吃饭 / 昨天晚上 / 我 / 回来 / 晚上九点 / 请我

(My friend took me out for dinner last night. I didn't come back until 9:00 p.m.)

_____

3. 您 / 回来 / 给我 / 方便 / 以后 / 打 / 要是 / 电话

(If it is convenient for you, please give me a call after you come back.)

_____

D. Translate the following exchanges into Chinese. (PRESENTATIONAL)

1. A: Do you know Miss Chang?

_____

    B: I don't know her.

_____

    A: This is a photo of Miss Chang.

_____

    B: She is tall and pretty. I'd like to meet her.

_____

    A: No problem. I'll call her now.

_____

    B: Great!

_____

2. A: I have a meeting tomorrow. Help me prepare, OK?

_____

    B: Sure, I will help you after dinner. Could you wait a bit?

_____

    A: Okay, I'll wait for you.

_____

3. **A:** When are you free today?

_____

B: I have three classes today, and won't be free until after 2:30 p.m. What's the

matter?

_____

A: I'd like to ask you to practice Chinese with me.

_____

B: Okay, I'll wait for you at the library at 3:00 p.m.

_____

E. Write an e-mail message to your Chinese friend to see if he/she can practice Chinese with you tomorrow evening. Promise him/her that you will buy him/her a cup of coffee afterwards. (PRESENTATIONAL)

F. Plan a perfect date. Indicate where and when you wish to meet with your date, and list what you would like to do by using the sentence pattern "A 跟 B + V(O)." (PRESENTATIONAL)

LESSON 7 Studying Chinese

第七课   学中文

PART ONE ## Dialogue I: How Did You Do on the Exam?

🔊 ## I. Listening Comprehension (INTERPRETIVE)

A. Textbook Dialogue (True/False)

( ) **1.**   Li You didn't do well on her test last week.

( ) **2.**   Wang Peng writes Chinese characters well, but very slowly.

( ) **3.**   Wang Peng didn't want to teach Li You how to write Chinese characters.

( ) **4.**   Li You has gone over tomorrow's lesson.

( ) **5.**   The Chinese characters in Lesson Seven are very easy.

( ) **6.**   Li You has no problems with Lesson Seven's grammar.

B. Workbook Narrative (True/False)

( ) **1.**   Mr. Li likes studying Chinese, but not English.

( ) **2.**   Mr. Li feels that English grammar is not too difficult, but Chinese grammar is hard.

( ) **3.**   Mr. Li has some difficulties with Chinese characters.

C. Workbook Dialogue (True/False)

( ) **1.**   The woman didn't do very well on the Chinese test last week.

( ) **2.**   The woman confessed that she spent a lot of time watching TV.

( ) **3.**   The man thinks that the woman should have been more prepared.

( ) **4.**   The woman thinks that the man was too busy to help her.

II. Speaking Exercises

A. Answer the questions in Chinese based on the Textbook Dialogue. (INTERPRETIVE AND PRESENTATIONAL)

1. How did Li You do on last week's test? Why?
2. Why does Wang Peng offer to help Li You with her writing of Chinese characters?
3. Who writes Chinese characters quickly?
4. Which lesson will Li You study tomorrow?
5. How does Li You feel about the grammar, vocabulary and characters in the lesson she has prepared?
6. What will Wang Peng and Li You do tonight?

B. Comment on how you feel about the grammar, vocabulary and characters of the last lesson you studied. (PRESENTATIONAL)

C. Discuss the result of your recent Chinese test with your partner. Comment on how you did in learning the grammar, reviewing the vocabulary and writing the characters. (INTERPERSONAL)

III. Reading Comprehension (INTERPRETIVE)

A. This is a note that Little Bai left for Little Wang. Read it and answer the questions. (True/False)

小王：

　　你好！我上个星期有个中文考试，我考得不太好。我写汉字写得不错，可是太慢。中文语法也有一点儿难，我不太懂。这个周末你有时间吗？我想请你帮我复习中文。好吗？

　　　　　　　　　　　　　　　　　　　　　　　　小白

Questions:

( ) **1.** Little Bai did a good job on the exam.
( ) **2.** Little Bai wrote the characters pretty well, although she did not write quickly.
( ) **3.** Little Bai didn't understand the grammar at all.
( ) **4.** Little Bai hoped to see Little Wang this afternoon.
( ) **5.** Little Wang's Chinese seems to be better than Little Bai's.

B. Read the following passage written by a student and answer the questions below. (True/False)

我们都不喜欢考试，但是我们的中文老师常常给我们考试。我们喜欢唱歌、跳舞，可是我们的老师不唱歌、也不跳舞，很没有意思。她说我们得常常听中文、练习说中文。要是我们听了，练习了，她很高兴。要是我们没听、没练习，她很不高兴。有的时候，我们还得去她的办公室请她帮我们复习。要是老师不来学校上课，不给我们考试，要是老师在家喝茶、看电视、聊天，那不是很好吗？

Questions:

( ) **1.** The narrator considers her attitude toward tests representative of her fellow students.

( ) **2.** The teacher is popular because she and the students have similar hobbies.

( ) **3.** The teacher seems to care very much about the students' effort in learning.

( ) **4.** The students often have tea with the teacher in her office.

( ) **5.** The teacher has decided not to give tests to the students anymore.

( ) **6.** The narrator hopes the teacher will invite the students to visit her home.

C. Read the passage and answer the questions. (True/False)

昨天是小高的生日，李友和王朋都到小高家去了。他们一起喝茶，听音乐，唱歌，晚上十二点才回家。王朋因为喝了很多茶，所以睡觉睡得不好。李友因为昨天没有准备，所以今天的考试她考得不好。

Questions:

( ) **1.** Both Wang Peng and Li You went to Little Gao's place.

( ) **2.** Yesterday evening, Wang Peng, Li You, and Little Gao were all out.

( ) **3.** Wang Peng was the only one who drank tea last night.

( ) **4.** Wang Peng didn't sleep well last night because he had too much cola.

( ) **5.** Li You didn't have time yesterday to prepare for today's test.

D. This is the title of a book. Would you be interested in reading this book? Why or why not?

实用现代汉语语法

IV. Writing and Grammar Exercises

A. Draw a line connecting the object with its proper measure word. (INTERPRETIVE)

一位　　　　一杯　　　　一瓶　　　　一枝　　　　一张

B. What kinds of praise have you received or would you like to receive from your teacher, friends, or classmate? List them by using 得.

EXAMPLE: 说中文/好　　　　　→　你说中文说得很好。

1. 打球/很好　　　　　→　_____ 。

2. 写字/漂亮　　　　　→　_____ 。

3. 说英文/快　　　　　→　_____ 。

4. 考试/好　　　　　　→　_____ 。

5. 预习生词语法/不错　→　_____ 。

C. Do you know how to say "to give someone something"? Let's practice with the help of the visuals. (PRESENTATIONAL)

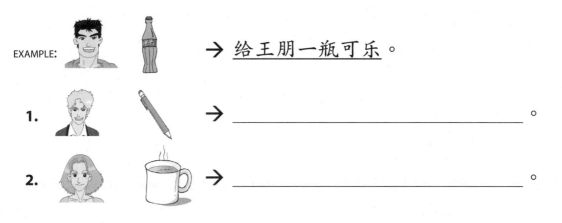

EXAMPLE:　　　　　→　给王朋一瓶可乐。

1. 　　　　　→　_____ 。

2. 　　　　　→　_____ 。

3. → _____ 。

4. → _____ 。

D. Fill in the blanks with the words given. Each word can only be used once. (INTERPRETIVE AND PRESENTATIONAL)

| 1. 太 | 2. 有一点儿 | 3. 都 | 4. 也 | 5. 一起 | 6. 常常 | 7. 可是 |

我和我的姐姐_____喜欢听音乐。我们_____ _____听。我们_____喜欢学中文。_____中国人说中文说得_____快。我觉得语法也_____难。

E. Which of the following tasks are important or urgent enough that you think you should do them right away? Select two. (INTERPRETIVE)

EXAMPLE: If you choose number 3, 给爸爸打电话,

you will write: 我<u>现在</u><u>就</u>给爸爸打电话。

1. 去同学家玩儿	2. 跟男/女朋友见面	3. 给爸爸打电话
4. 跟妈妈说话	5. 回家睡觉	6. 去学校开会
7. 练习说中文	8. 练习写汉字	9. 准备考试
10. 预习生词语法		

_____

_____

F. Translate the following exchanges into Chinese. (PRESENTATIONAL)

1. **A:** I think Chinese is interesting.

    _____

    B: But I feel that Chinese grammar is a bit hard.

    _____

2. **A:** How about you teach me how to write characters?

    _____

    B: Okay, give me a pen. Let's do it now.

    _____

3. **A:** How did you do on the test?

    _____

    B: I reviewed Lesson Six well, so I tested well.

    _____

4. **A:** You write Chinese characters way too slowly.

    _____

    B: You speak Chinese way too slowly.

    _____

5. **A:** Could you help me to practice speaking Chinese?

    _____

    B: I speak Chinese poorly. Let's go to the teacher's office and ask the teacher to help us.

    _____

    A: Okay. We'll go find him now.

    _____

G. Comment on how well or how badly your family, classmates, friends or any celebrities do the following activities. (PRESENTATIONAL)

EXAMPLE: 我觉得姚明(Yáo Míng)打球打得不错。

1. 打球 _____

2. 唱歌 _____

3. 跳舞 _____

4. 工作 _____

5. 说英文 _____

6. 学中文 _____

7. 预习生词语法 _____

8. 准备考试 _____

Dialogue II: Preparing for a Chinese Class

PART TWO

 I. Listening Comprehension (INTERPRETIVE)

A. Textbook Dialogue (True/False)

( ) **1.**   Bai Ying'ai is always late.

( ) **2.**   Bai Ying'ai didn't go to bed until early this morning.

( ) **3.**   Li You went to bed very late, because she was studying Chinese.

( ) **4.**   Li You recited the lesson well, because she listened to the recording the night before.

( ) **5.**   According to Bai Ying'ai, Li You has a very handsome Chinese friend.

B. Workbook Dialogue (True/False)

( ) **1.**   The man usually comes early.

( ) **2.**   The man previewed Lesson Eight.

( ) **3.**   The man went to bed early because he didn't have homework last night.

( ) **4.**   The man usually goes to bed around 9:00 p.m.

II. Speaking Exercises

A. Answer the questions in Chinese based on the Textbook Dialogue. (INTERPRETIVE AND PRESENTATIONAL)

1.   Why did Bai Ying'ai come so late today?
2.   Why was Li You able to go to bed early last night?
3.   Why did Bai Ying'ai say that it is nice to have a Chinese friend?
4.   Which lesson is the class studying today?
5.   Who did not listen to the recording last night?
6.   How did Bai Ying'ai describe Li You's friend?

B. You and your partner will participate in a simulated conversation. (INTERPERSONAL)

1.   Find out if your partner was late or early for class;
2.   Find out if your partner went to bed early or late;
3.   Find out if your partner prepared for today's lesson.

III. Reading Comprehension (INTERPRETIVE)

A. Read Li You's schedule for today and answer the questions. (True/False)

上午	八点半	预习生词
	九点一刻	听录音
	十点	上中文课
中午	十二点	吃午饭
下午	一点	睡觉
	两点	复习中文
晚上	六点	吃晚饭
	八点	做功课

Questions:

( ) **1.** 李友今天没有课。

( ) **2.** 李友上午预习生词。

( ) **3.** 李友下午听录音。

( ) **4.** 李友不吃午饭，只吃晚饭。

( ) **5.** 李友复习中文以后睡午觉。

( ) **6.** 李友吃晚饭以后做功课。

B. Read the passage and answer the questions. (True/False)

今天上午，小李预习了第六课。第六课的语法有点儿难，生词也很多。下午她要去老师的办公室问问题。她觉得学中文很有意思。说中国话不太难，可是汉字有一点儿难。

Questions:

( ) **1.** Little Li thinks Lesson 6 is not easy.

( ) **2.** Little Li will go to her teacher's office today.

( ) **3.** Little Li's teacher will give her a test this afternoon.

( ) **4.** Little Li feels very frustrated with her Chinese.

( ) **5.** Little Li considers speaking Chinese easier than writing Chinese characters.

C. Read the passage and answer the questions below.

　　小美是中国学生，在美国大学学英文。昨天下午她在图书馆做功课。她觉得英文生词太多，语法也不容易。一个美国男学生帮她复习生词和语法，所以她做功课做得很快。那个美国男生很帅，很酷。今天小美想给他打电话，才知道没有问他的名字和电话。

Questions: (Multiple Choice)

( ) **1.** Which of the statements is true about Xiao Mei?

   a. She is a Chinese student tutoring American students in Chinese.
   b. She is an American student taking a Chinese class.
   c. She is a Chinese student taking an English class.
   d. She is an American student studying Chinese with Chinese students.

( ) **2.** Which of the statements is true about her homework yesterday?

   a. She completed it quickly because the grammar and vocabulary were easy.
   b. She completed it quickly even though the grammar and vocabulary were difficult.
   c. She completed it slowly because the grammar and vocabulary were difficult.
   d. She completed it slowly even though the grammar and vocabulary were easy.

Questions: (True/False)

( ) **3.** We can assume that Xiao Mei likes the young man she met.

( ) **4.** Xiao Mei had the young man's phone number.

D. These are book titles. How many of them are on Chinese grammar and how many are on Chinese characters?

IV. Writing and Grammar Exercises

A. When people praise or complain, they often use 真 or 太. Fill in the blanks with the appropriate word.

1. 老师说话说得＿＿＿慢了，学生都不想听。

2. 功课＿＿＿多，晚上得听录音、写汉字。

3. 早上七点半就得去学校上课，＿＿＿早了。

4. 你哥哥＿＿＿帅，很多女孩子都想认识他。

5. 小王写汉字写得＿＿＿漂亮，我想请他教我怎么写。

6. 你念课文念得＿＿＿不错，常常听录音吧？

7. 李老师上课上得＿＿＿好了，大家都喜欢上他的课。

B. Answer the following questions according to your own circumstances. (INTERPERSONAL)

EXAMPLE: A: 你昨天睡觉睡得晚吗？ B: <u>我睡觉睡得很晚/不晚</u>。

1. **A:** 你写字写得快吗？

   B: _____ 。

2. **A:** 你唱歌唱得好吗？

   B: _____ 。

3. **A:** 你打球打得好吗？

   B: _____ 。

4. **A:** 你跳舞跳得怎么样？

   B: _____ 。

5. **A:** 你念课文念得怎么样？

   B: _____ 。

C. Last week Little Li was either late or early. Complete the following sentences with either 才 or 就.

EXAMPLE: 学校下午三点开会   2:00 p.m.

→ 学校下午三点开会，小李两点<u>就</u>来了。

1. 我们昨天上午九点钟考试   8:45 a.m.

→ _____ 。

2. 我们星期一去老师办公室问问题   Wednesday

→ _____ 。

3. 我们星期四预习生词语法   Tuesday

→ _____ 。

4. 我们昨天晚上十点回家   11:30

→ _____ 。

D. Translate the following exchanges into Chinese. (PRESENTATIONAL)

1. **A:** How come you have so much homework tonight?

_____

B: The teacher is going to give us a test tomorrow, and I have to review the text and practice writing Chinese.

_____

2. **A:** Did you prepare Lesson 8 last night?

_____

B: No, I didn't. I went to bed as early as 9:30.

_____

A: That was indeed early. I didn't go to bed until 1:30.

_____

B: That's way too late.

_____

3. **A:** This is my boyfriend's picture.

_____

B: He is very handsome.

_____

A: He sings well, dances well, and plays ball well.

_____

B: That's so cool!

_____

E. Are you a fan of someone? List the names of your idols and describe why you think they are so cool. (PRESENTATIONAL)

EXAMPLE: If you are a fan of Yao Ming, you might want to say

姚明真酷，他打球打得真好。

F. Translate the following passage into Chinese: (PRESENTATIONAL)

My younger sister did not learn Chinese well. She didn't like listening to recordings and didn't practice speaking, so she did not speak well. She didn't like studying grammar or writing characters. That was why she didn't do well on examinations. But after she met a Chinese friend, she often reviewed Chinese with her Chinese friend in the library. Now, she likes listening to the audio recordings and she also writes characters pretty well.

LESSON 8 School Life

第八课　学校生活

PART ONE A Diary: A Typical School Day

I. Listening Comprehension (INTERPRETIVE)

A. The Textbook Diary (Multiple Choice)

( ) **1.** Which day of the week is November 3rd?

　　a. Monday　　　**b.** Tuesday　　　**c.** Wednesday　　　**d.** Thursday

( ) **2.** What did Li You do this morning before breakfast?

　　a. She took a bath.
　　b. She listened to the recording.
　　c. She read the newspaper.
　　d. She talked to her friend on the phone.

( ) **3.** What time did Li You go to class this morning?

　　a. 7:30　　　**b.** 8:00　　　**c.** 8:30　　　**d.** 9:00

( ) **4.** What did Li You *not* do in her Chinese class?

　　a. Take a test.
　　b. Practice pronunciation.
　　c. Learn vocabulary.
　　d. Study grammar.

( ) **5.** Where did Li You have lunch today?

　　a. At a Chinese restaurant.
　　b. At the school cafeteria.
　　c. At home.
　　d. At her friend's house.

( ) **6.** What was Li You doing around 4:30 p.m.?

    a. Practicing Chinese.

    b. Reading a newspaper.

    c. Playing ball.

    d. Drinking coffee.

( ) **7.** What time did Li You eat her dinner?

    a. 5:45   **b.** 6:00   **c.** 6:30   **d.** 7:30

( ) **8.** Li You went to Bai Ying'ai's dorm to:

    a. eat dinner   **b.** read the newspaper   **c.** chat   **d.** study

( ) **9.** What time did Li You return to her place?

    a. 7:30   **b.** 8:30   **c.** 9:30   **d.** 10:30

( ) **10.** What did Li You do before she went to bed?

    a. Visited Little Bai.

    b. Did her homework.

    c. Talked to Wang Peng on the phone.

    d. Prepared for her test.

B. Use the numbers 1–3 to put the pictures in the correct sequence based on the information given in the Diary.

_____ _____ _____

C. Workbook Dialogue I (True/False)

( ) **1.** Li You is going to Teacher Zhang's office at 4:00 p.m. today.

( ) **2.** Wang Peng will be attending a class at 2:30 p.m. today.

( ) **3.** Li You plans to surf the net in the library this evening.

( ) **4.** Li You and Wang Peng will see each other in the library this evening.

II. Speaking Exercises

A. Answer the questions in Chinese based on the Textbook Diary. (INTERPRETIVE AND PRESENTATIONAL)

1. What did Li You do after getting up?
2. Did Li You have breakfast?
3. How many classes did Li You have?
4. What did the teacher do in Li You's first class?
5. What did Li You do during the lunch hour?
6. What did Li You do in the library?
7. What did Li You do after dinner?

B. With a partner, participate in a simulated conversation. Look at the schedule given and take turns with your partner to describe what Wang Peng did yesterday morning. (INTERPERSONAL)

8:45 a.m.

III. Reading Comprehension

A. Read the following schedule for Little Wang and answer the questions. (True/False) (INTERPRETIVE)

8:00	复习第七课生词、语法
9:00	上电脑课
10:00	去常老师的办公室练习发音
14:30	去图书馆看报
16:00	去打球
18:00	去宿舍餐厅吃晚饭
20:15	给小李打电话，跟他一起练习中文
22:30	给爸爸妈妈打电话
24:00	睡觉

Questions:

( ) **1.** 小王今天只有一节课。

( ) **2.** 小王跟小白一起吃午饭。

( ) **3.** 小王上午去找常老师。

( ) **4.** 小王去小李家练习中文。

( ) **5.** 小王吃晚饭以前去打球。

( ) **6.** 小王去图书馆以后去找常老师。

( ) **7.** 小王睡觉以前给爸爸妈妈打电话。

( ) **8.** 小王跟小李练习中文以后才吃饭。

B. Read the passage and answer the questions. (True/False)

小高以前常常跟朋友一起打球，聊天，看电视，不做功课。可是因为他下星期要考试，所以这个星期他不打球，不看电视，也不找朋友聊天，一个人到图书馆去看书。他很早就起床，很晚才睡觉，所以他上课的时候常常想睡觉。

Questions:

( ) **1.** 小高以前常常跟朋友一边做功课，一边聊天。

( ) **2.** 小高常常跟朋友一起到图书馆去看书。

( ) **3.** 因为小高要准备考试，所以他这个星期很忙。

( ) **4.** 小高觉得上课没有意思，所以他上课的时候常常想睡觉。

( ) **5.** 这个星期小高睡觉睡得很早。

C. Read the dialogue and answer the questions. (True/False)

小李：你认识小常的男朋友文书明吗？

小白：我认识。昨天我去图书馆上网的时候，他正在跟小常一起做

功课。

小李：我也认识他，因为他跟我一起上电脑课。

小白：我觉得他很酷！

小李：他很帅，可是我不太喜欢他。

小白：是吗？为什么？

小李：别人说他有的时候一边给小常打电话，一边给别的女孩子写信。

小白：是吗？小常知道不知道？你得告诉她！

Questions:

( ) **1.** Little Bai is Little Chang's friend, but Little Li is not.
( ) **2.** Little Bai is in the same computer class as Wen Shuming.
( ) **3.** Little Chang and Wen Shuming did their homework together yesterday.
( ) **4.** Little Bai saw Little Li in the library yesterday.
( ) **5.** Little Li thinks Wen Shuming is handsome, but does not like him.
( ) **6.** At the end of the dialogue, Little Bai wants Little Li to talk to Little Chang.

IV. Writing and Grammar Exercises (PRESENTATIONAL)

A. Wang Peng is very talented. He has many skills and is happy to help his friends. Based on the visuals provided, state what he can teach his friends.

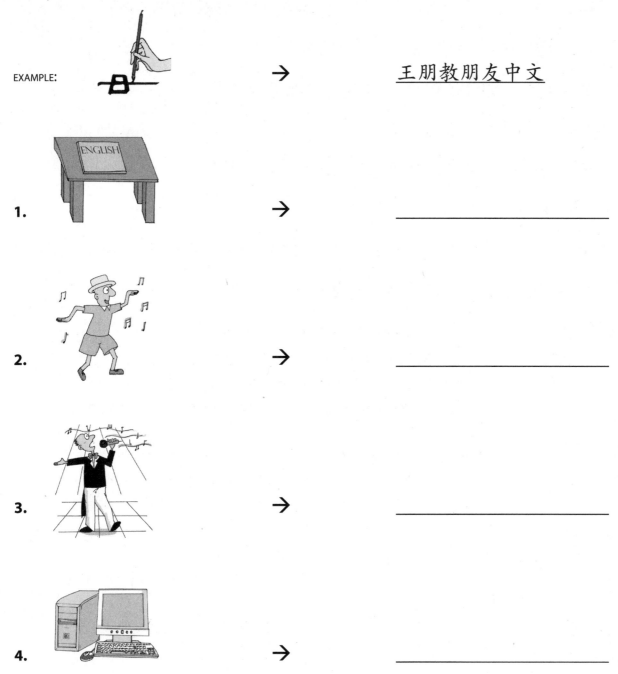

EXAMPLE: →   <u>王朋教朋友中文</u>

1.   →   _____

2.   →   _____

3.   →   _____

4.   →   _____

B. Nowadays, people can multi-task. Doing two things at the same time is no big deal. Let's look at what they are doing.

EXAMPLE: → 他一边儿吃早饭，一边儿看电视

1. → _____

2. → _____

3. → _____

4. → _____

C. Describe what people are doing based on the visuals given.

EXAMPLE: → <u>他正在上课</u>

1. → _____

2. → _____

3. → _____

4. → _____

5. → _____

D. Translate the following exchanges into Chinese.

1. **A:** What do you want to do after class?

    _____

    B: I want to go back to the dorm to do homework.

    _____

2. **A:** You speak Chinese so well. Could you help me practice before tomorrow's test?

    _____

    B: No problem. Let's have coffee and practice at the same time.

    _____

3. **A:** This new text is a bit difficult.

    _____

    B: Let's ask the teacher when we meet her tomorrow.

    _____

4. **A:** I'll go to the cafeteria to have lunch right after the test. Have you had lunch already?

    _____

    B: Don't wait for me. I have to work. I don't know when I'll have lunch today.

    _____

E. You are a newly hired personal assistant. You need to find out what your new boss's daily routine is in order to plan his schedule better. You need to find out:

  1. when your boss gets up in the morning;
  2. whether he takes his shower in the morning after he gets up or before he goes to bed in the evening;
  3. whether he prefers to have breakfast at home or in the office;
  4. when and with whom he has regular meetings;
  5. what time he has his lunches and dinners;
  6. when he cannot be disturbed;
  7. what time he plans to return home after work;
  8. what time he goes to bed;
9–10. and any other daily activities that should be included in the appointment book.

After gathering all the information, you now need to input it into the Chinese PDA.

1. _____

2. _____

3. _____

4. _____

5. _____

6. _____

7. _____

8. _____

9. _____

10. _____

F. Write a diary entry in Chinese about your daily routine.

PART TWO   A Letter: Talking about Studying Chinese

🔘 I. Listening Comprehension (INTERPRETIVE)

A. The Textbook Letter (True/False)

( ) **1.** This is a letter from Li You to Wang Peng.

( ) **2.** Li You's major is Chinese.

( ) **3.** Li You does not like her Chinese class at all.

( ) **4.** Li You's Chinese teacher speaks English very well.

( ) **5.** Li You is learning Chinese quickly, because she has some help.

( ) **6.** Li You would like her friend to attend her school concert.

B. Workbook Narrative I (True/False)

( ) **1.** Wang Peng went to the library to help Li You with her Chinese.

( ) **2.** Wang Peng did not go to play ball this afternoon until he had finished his homework.

( ) **3.** Li You went to a movie with Wang Peng this evening.

( ) **4.** Li You has a Chinese class tomorrow.

C. Workbook Narrative II

Listen to the passage that describes Little Li's activities yesterday, and then place the letters representing those activities to the right column in the correct order.

a.

1. _____

b.

2. _____

c.

3. _____

d.

4. _____

e.

5. _____

f.

6. _____

g.

7. _____

h.

8. _____

II. Speaking Exercises

A. Answer the questions in Chinese based on Li You's letter in the textbook. (INTERPRETIVE AND PRESENTATIONAL)

1. Why is Li You so busy this semester?
2. Describe Li You's Chinese class.
3. How did Li You feel about her Chinese class? Why?
4. Why did Li You ask Xiaoyin if she liked music?

B. Describe your Chinese class to your friend in great detail. Make sure to comment on how you feel about pronunciation, grammar, vocabulary, and Chinese characters. (PRESENTATIONAL)

III. Reading Comprehension

A. Read the following email message and answer questions. (Multiple Choice) (INTERPRETIVE)

文书明：

　　你好！谢谢你那天在图书馆帮我复习英文语法。我的英文不好，请你别笑我。那天我不知道你的名字，但是后来我的朋友告诉我，你有一个漂亮的中文名字。我还知道，你这个学期除了电脑专业课以外，还在学中文。这个周末有一个中国电影，希望你能来看。有空的时候给我打个电话，好吗？我的电话是555-5555。

小美

Questions:

( ) **1.** Xiao Mei still feels rather _____ about her English.

    a. frustrated　　**b.** embarrassed　　**c.** proud

( ) **2.** Where did Xiao Mei get the information about Wen Shuming?

    a. From Wen Shuming himself
    b. From the librarian
    c. From her friends

( ) **3.** According to Xiao Mei, Wen Shuming is _____.

    a. a computer science major who studies Chinese

    b. a Chinese major who studies computer science

    c. a student who majors in Chinese and computer science

( ) **4.** Little Mei hopes that Wen Shuming will _____.

    a. come to see the movie but not call her

    b. call her but not come to the movie

    c. call her and come to the movie

B. Read the passage and answer the questions. (True/False)

小高今天很忙，上午除了有三节课以外，还有一个电脑考试。中午跟朋友一起吃饭，下午在图书馆看书，做功课，晚上在电脑室上网聊天儿，十点才回家吃晚饭。晚饭以后，他一边看电视，一边预习明天的功课，十二点半才睡觉。

Questions:

( ) **1.** 小高上午没空。

( ) **2.** 小高下午不在家，在图书馆工作。

( ) **3.** 小高晚上很晚才吃饭。

( ) **4.** 小高晚上在电脑室预习明天的功课。

( ) **5.** 小高一边听音乐，一边看书。

C. Based on your reading of the passage below, list five ways in which you are similar to or different from the narrator. Write your statements in English, and start each statement with the phrase "Like the person" or "Unlike the person."

我是大学一年级的学生。开始我不知道教室在哪儿，因为学校太大了；我不喜欢吃学校餐厅的饭，因为餐厅的饭太不好吃了；我也不会用学校图书馆的电脑，因为图书馆的电脑太新了。在宿舍洗澡也很不方便。中文课很难。除了生词太多以外，我还觉得老师说话说得太快。

1. _____
2. _____
3. _____
4. _____
5. _____

IV. Writing and Grammar Exercises

A. Fill in the blanks with the appropriate measure words. Each measure word can only be used once.

1. 一_____老师
2. 一_____照片
3. 一_____电脑
4. 一_____笔
5. 一_____咖啡
6. 一_____可乐
7. 一_____课
8. 一_____日记
9. 一_____信
10. 我家有三_____人。

B. Answer the following questions involving tools, methods, or means. (INTERPERSONAL AND PRESENTATIONAL)

EXAMPLE: **A:** 高文中用什么做功课？

→ **B:** <u>他用电脑做功课。</u>

1. **A:** 白英爱怎么学发音？

→ **B:** _____

2. **A:** 李友用什么练习写汉字？

→ **B:** _____

3. **A:** 高小音用中文还是英文写日记？

→ **B:** _____

C. Bai Ying'ai is such a capable person. She has many skills, and there is only one thing she is not able to handle. List some of the things that she can do and the only thing she cannot do based on the information given. (PRESENTATIONAL)

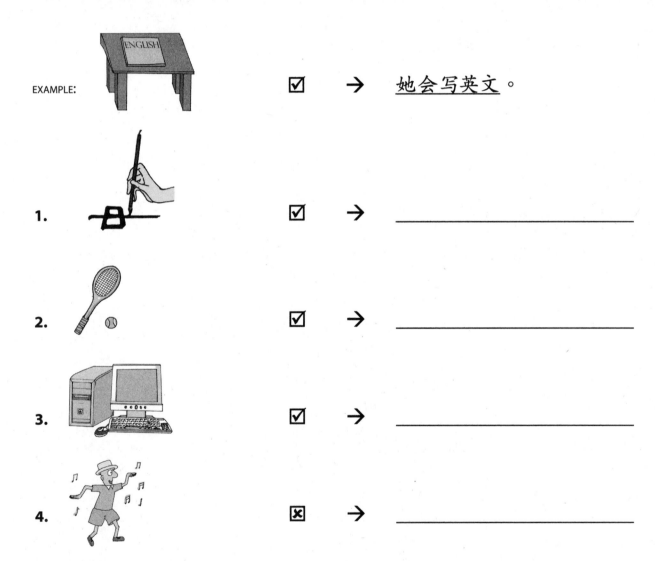

EXAMPLE: ☑ →   她会写英文。

1.   ☑ → _____

2.   ☑ → _____

3.   ☑ → _____

4.   ☒ → _____

D. According to our parents and teachers, there are some things that we are not supposed to do at home or in class. Can you think of some of those things with the help of the visuals? (INTERPRETIVE AND PRESENTATIONAL)

EXAMPLE: 老师告诉我，考试的时候，。

→ 老师告诉我，考试的时候，<u>不能问问题</u>。

1. 老师告诉我，上课的时候，。

_____

2. 老师告诉我，上课的时候，。

_____

3. 妈妈告诉我，做功课的时候，。

_____

4. 妈妈告诉我，吃饭的时候，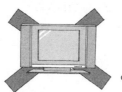。

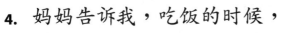

E. Follow the model and combine the sentences in each group into one that contains the structure "除了...以外，还".

EXAMPLE: 喜欢 +

→ <u>高文中除了喜欢唱歌以外，还喜欢跳舞。</u>

1. 教 +

→ _____

2. 喝 +

→ _____

3. 会 +

→ _____

F. Translate the following exchanges into Chinese. (PRESENTATIONAL)

1. **A:** What are you doing?

_____

B: I am writing a letter to my friend.

_____

A: Really? Are you writing it in English or Chinese?

_____

B: I'm writing it in Chinese. She doesn't know English.

_____

2. **A:** Did Teacher Chang help you practice speaking Chinese yesterday?

_____

B: No. She was at a meeting when I got to her office.

_____

3. **A:** What's your major?

_____

B: My major is computer (science).

_____

A: Great! Can you teach me how to go online?

_____

B: Okay, I'll help you right after my class.

_____

4. **A:** You write characters so quickly.

_____

B: At first, I wrote very slowly. But later, my big brother helped me practice. Now I write quickly.

_____

5. **A:** Tomorrow is the weekend. I hope you can go to a concert with me.

_____

B: I am sorry. I cannot go. I have to work.

_____

6. **A:** This grammar is a bit difficult. Do you understand it?

_____

B: Don't ask me, I don't understand it either.

_____

G. Write down what Little Wang did yesterday based on the visuals provided. (PRESENTATIONAL)

小王的一天

H. Write your friend a letter in Chinese. Tell him/her about your experience of learning Chinese. Please include information on your study habits, in-class situation, after-class work, your strengths and weaknesses, and your likes and dislikes. Please also comment on how your instructor teaches or how your classmates study. Don't forget to ask your friend about his/her studies, and wish him/her the best. (PRESENTATIONAL)

LESSON 9   **Shopping**
第九课   买东西

PART ONE   **Dialogue I: Shopping for Clothes**

I. Listening Comprehension (INTERPRETIVE)

A. Textbook Dialogue (Multiple Choice)

( ) **1.**   What color shirt did Li You want to buy?

    a. black   **b.** white   **c.** red   **d.** yellow

( ) **2.**   What else did Li You want to buy besides the shirt?

    a. a hat   **b.** a pair of shoes   **c.** a sweater   **d.** a pair of pants

( ) **3.**   What size did Li You wear?

    a. small   **b.** medium   **c.** large   **d.** extra-large

( ) **4.**   How much did Li You need to pay altogether?

    a. between $20 and $30
    b. between $30 and $40
    c. between $40 and $50
    d. between $50 and $60

B. Workbook Narrative (Multiple Choice)

( ) **1.**   What color does Wang Peng like?

    a. blue   **b.** brown   **c.** white   **d.** red

( ) **2.**   Why does Wang Peng not like the shirt? Because of its _____.

    a. price   **b.** style   **c.** color   **d.** size

( )**3.** What colors did the salesperson say they had?

    a. white, blue, and brown

    b. white, red, and brown

    c. red, blue, and white

    d. white, red, and yellow

( )**4.** When did Wang Peng buy the shirt?

    a. 5 days ago.   **b.** 7 days ago.   **c.** 10 days ago.   **d.** 14 days ago.

II. Speaking Exercises

A. Answer the questions in Chinese based on the Textbook Dialogue. (INTERPRETIVE AND PRESENTATIONAL)

    1. What did Li You want to buy?

    2. What color did Li You like?

    3. What did Li You like about the pants?

    4. Give the price for each item, and the total cost.

B. With a partner, participate in a simulated conversation. Ask each other what size shirt/pants you wear, what color you prefer, and the price of the top you are wearing. (INTERPERSONAL)

III. Reading Comprehension (INTERPRETIVE)

A. Read the following passage and answer the questions. (True/False)

    小文上个周末去买东西。他想买一件中号的红衬衫，可是中号衬衫都是白的，红衬衫都是大号的。售货员很客气。她帮小文找了一件衬衫，不是红的，可是颜色不错。那位售货员告诉他，这件衬衫三十九块九毛九。小文觉得有一点儿贵，可是他觉得要是不买就对不起那位售货员，所以给了售货员四十块钱买了那件衬衫。

Questions:

( ) **1.** There were many choices in the store for Little Wen to select from.

( ) **2.** The salesperson was very courteous.

( ) **3.** Little Wen probably wears a size medium shirt.

( ) **4.** Little Wen was looking for a white shirt.

( ) **5.** Finally the salesperson found a red shirt that Little Wen liked.

( ) **6.** Little Wen bought the shirt because he didn't want to disappoint the salesperson.

B. Read the dialogue and answer the questions. (True/False)

男：我今天买了一件衬衫，你看怎么样？

女：大小很合适，可是颜色不太好。你喜欢穿红衬衫，怎么买了这个
    颜色的？

男：我想买红的，可是红衬衫都太大了。

女：那你为什么买这件？

男：因为那位售货员…

女：很漂亮，对不对？

男：不、不、不。她不认识我，但是我知道她是你的朋友。

女：是吗？

Questions:

( ) **1.** The woman liked the color but not the size of the man's new shirt.

( ) **2.** The woman was somewhat surprised that the man bought that shirt.

( ) **3.** We can assume that many of the man's shirts were red.

( ) **4.** The man bought the shirt because the price was right.

( ) **5.** The salesperson turned out to be the man's friend.

C. This is an index of classified ads from a Chinese newspaper. According to the index, on what page can you find ads for apparel?

专项分类资讯 ▶ ▶ ▶		
二手房超市、租房手册	音像软件	79版
36版	家居建材	81版
美好姻缘 54版	健康专递	82版
招生广场 66、69版	服装服饰	82版
美容美发招生 67版	五金、机械、化工	83版
择业直通车 70、71版	印刷设计	83版
留学与移民 72版	快乐京郊游	84版
汽车服务 75版	天天美容	84版

IV. Writing and Grammar Exercises (PRESENTATIONAL)

A. How much do these things cost in your city?

EXAMPLE: → **A:** 一瓶可乐多少钱？

B: 一瓶可乐两块九毛九分钱。

1. _____

2. _____

3. _____

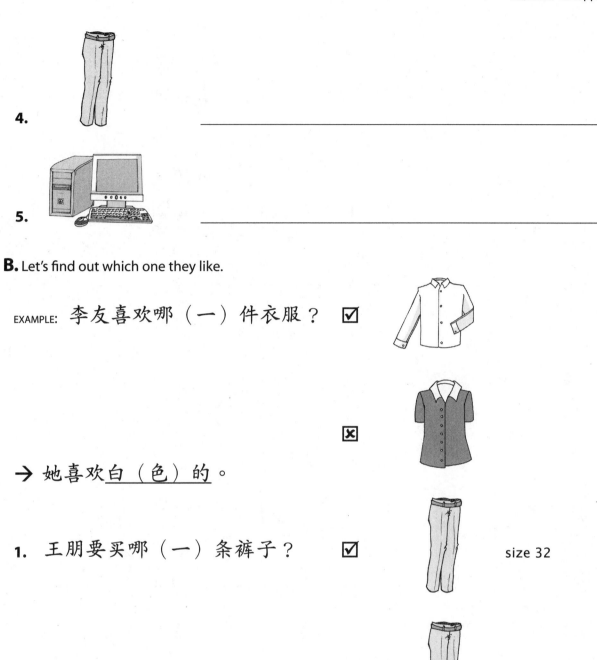

4. _____

5. _____

B. Let's find out which one they like.

EXAMPLE: 李友喜欢哪（一）件衣服？ ☑

☒

→ 她喜欢白（色）的。

1. 王朋要买哪（一）条裤子？ ☑

size 32

☒

size 34

→ _____

2. 高小音想喝什么茶？ ☒  tea $3.50

☑  tea $2.00

→ _____

3. 白英爱用哪枝笔？ ☒

☑

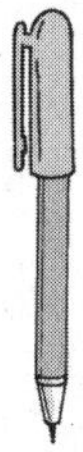

→ _____

C. Translate the following exchanges into Chinese.

1. **A:** This shirt is so pretty. Try it on.

_____

B: There's no need to. It's too expensive.

_____

2. **A:** What size pants do you wear?

_____

B: I wear size 30.

_____

3. **A:** Both the color and the length of the pants are right for you. Get them!

_____

B: I'll buy them if they are cheap.

_____

4. **A:** Miss, excuse me, how much is this medium size shirt?

_____

B: It's twenty-nine dollars and fifty cents.

_____

A: Here's thirty dollars.

_____

B: Here's your change, fifty cents. Thank you.

_____

D. Look at an online clothing catalog. List the items you like. Include the colors and prices. Don't forget to bring a printout of the items you like to show your classmates and instructor.

E. Describe what you are wearing. Don't forget to mention the colors and sizes.

PART TWO Dialogue II: Exchanging Shoes

I. Listening Comprehension (INTERPRETIVE)

A. Textbook Dialogue (Multiple Choice)

( ) **1.** Why did Wang Peng want to exchange the shoes?

    a. The shoes did not fit well.

    b. The shoes were damaged.

    c. He did not like the price.

    d. He did not like the color.

( ) **2.** What color did Wang Peng prefer?

    a. black   **b.** white   **c.** brown   **d.** red

( ) **3.** In what way was the new pair of shoes like the old pair? They were _____.

    a. the same size   **b.** the same color

    c. the same price   **d.** the same design

B. Workbook Dialogue I (True/False)

( ) **1.** The man returned his shirt for a different one, because he didn't like the color.

( ) **2.** The man finally bought a yellow shirt because he liked the color.

( ) **3.** All the large-size shirts in the store were yellow ones.

( ) **4.** A large-size shirt fit the man well.

C. Workbook Dialogue II (True/False)

( ) **1.** The store only sells clothes.

( ) **2.** The man knew what color and what size to get.

( ) **3.** The man asked the salesperson for consultation.

( ) **4.** The determining factor for the man to make the purchase was the color.

( ) **5.** The man didn't want to ruin the surprise for his girlfriend.

( ) **6.** The salesperson agreed with the man's choice.

II. Speaking Exercises

A. Answer the questions in Chinese based on the Textbook Dialogue. (INTERPRETIVE AND PRESENTATIONAL)

1. Why did Wang Peng want to return the shoes for a different pair?
2. Did Wang Peng like the black shoes? Why or why not?
3. What color of shoes did Wang Peng finally accept? Why?
4. Did Wang Peng pay any additional money for the new shoes? Why or why not?

B. Describe the clothes you are wearing today. Don't forget to mention the colors, sizes, and prices. (PRESENTATIONAL)

C. You and your partner do a role play. One of you is a salesperson in a clothing store, and the other is a customer trying to exchange a shirt that is too large. Make sure the customer gets the right size, color, and price. (INTERPERSONAL)

III. Reading Comprehension (INTERPRETIVE)

A. Find the items corresponding to the descriptions below. Place the correct letter in the parentheses next to its description.

1. 短裤 （ ） **2.** 长裤 （ ） **3.** 大衣 （ ） **4.** 衬衫 （ ） **5.** 鞋 （ ）

 a.   **b.**   **c.**    **d.**   **e.**

B. Read the passage and answer the questions. (True/False)

李太太很喜欢买便宜的衣服。虽然她的衣服很多，可是她觉得都不太合适。李先生跟他太太不一样。他不喜欢买东西，也不常常买东西。李先生只买大小长短和颜色都合适的衣服，所以，他的衣服虽然不多，可是他都喜欢。

Questions:

( ) **1.** 李太太觉得买东西很有意思。

( ) **2.** 李太太的衣服很多，也都很贵。

( ) **3.** 李太太的衣服大小和颜色都很合适。

( ) **4.** 李先生觉得买衣服没意思。

( ) **5.** 李先生买了很多衣服。

( ) **6.** 李先生的衣服不大也不小，不长也不短。

C. It's a common practice for department stores to put up sale signs when they are having a sale. The following is such a sign. Look at the sign, try to identify and circle the goods that are on sale, and explain (in either English or Chinese) what kinds of deals are offered.

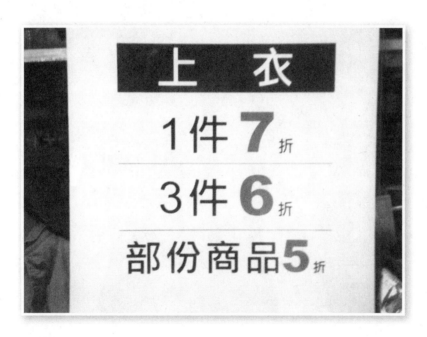

IV. Writing and Grammar Exercises

A. Draw a line from each object to its respective measure word. (INTERPRETIVE)

a. 位

b. 杯

c. 瓶

d. 封

e. 条

f. 张

g. 双

h. 枝

i. 件

B. Based on the texts, answer the following questions using "挺...的." (INTERPERSONAL)

EXAMPLE: **A:** 你觉得这一课的生词多不多？

B: <u>我觉得（这一课的生词）挺多的</u>。

1. **A:** 白英爱觉得王朋帅吗？

   B: _____

2. **A:** 王朋觉得李友漂亮吗？

   B: _____

3. **A:** 常老师觉得李友念课文念得怎么样？

   B: _____

4. **A:** 常老师觉得李友写汉字写得怎么样？

   B: _____

C. Follow the model and rewrite the following sentences using "A 跟 B 一样 + Adj."

EXAMPLE: 高文中今年十八岁，李友今年也十八岁。

→ <u>高文中跟李友一样大</u>。

1. 这件衬衫是中号的，那件衬衫也是中号的。

→ _____

2. 这双鞋五十块钱，那双鞋也五十块钱。

→ _____

3. 学中文很酷，学英文也很酷。

→ _____

4.   这个教室很新，那个教室也很新。

→ _____

5.   纽约很有意思，北京也很有意思。

→ _____

D. The following is a conversation between a salesperson and a customer, Miss Li. Complete the conversation based on the information given. (INTERPERSONAL)

售货员：_____？

李小姐：我想买一条裤子。

售货员：_____？

李小姐：大号的。

售货员：这条太大了，您可以换 _____。

李小姐：中号的长短、大小都很合适。

售货员：_____？

李小姐：还要买一双鞋。

售货员：_____？

李小姐：黄的。

售货员：一条裤子十九块，一双鞋十五块，一共_____。

李小姐：能不能_____？

售货员：对不起，我们不收_____。

李小姐：_____。

售货员：找您六十六块。

E. Translate the following exchanges into Chinese. (PRESENTATIONAL)

1. A: This store is quite nice. Their clothes are not too expensive.

_____

B: Although their clothes are not too expensive, they don't take credit cards. That's so inconvenient.

_____

_____

2. A: What size shirt do you wear?

_____

B: I wear medium.

_____

A: Do you like this red one? The style and the color are both right (for you).

_____

_____

B: I'll try it on.

_____

A: It's a little big (on you).

_____

B: Let's get a size small.

_____

3. A: I like to go shopping with my sister. She pays. I don't have to (pay).

_____

_____

B: Is that so? Your sister is so nice.

_____

4. A: I'd like to buy some pens. How much is a pen of this kind?

_____

_____

B: Three dollars each.

_____

A: Why so expensive? How about that kind?

_____

B: That kind is as expensive as this kind.

_____

F. Do you know your favorite celebrity well? Do a report on his/her fashion sense. Find out what size s/he wears and what color s/he likes. Locate a recent photo of your celebrity, and comment on whether the outfit s/he has on in the photo is right for her/him. In addition, provide some fashion advice to make your celebrity look even better. (PRESENTATIONAL)

G. Little Wang is trying to pick out an outfit for her party this weekend. But let's look at what she has on right now. Describe what she is wearing. Please provide information such as the color and the size of her clothing items, and her shoes. State how much each item costs. Comment on how Little Wang looks in this particular outfit, if you think the outfit suits her, and if it's too pricey, etc. (PRESENTATIONAL)

M $25.99 white

6 $37 black

7.5 $111.11 red

LESSON 10 **Transportation**

第十课 交通

PART ONE | Dialogue: Going Home for the Winter Vacation

I. Listening Comprehension (INTERPRETIVE)

A. The Textbook Dialogue (True/False)

( ) **1.** Li You will be leaving on the 21st.

( ) **2.** Li You should reach the airport no later than 8 o'clock in the morning.

( ) **3.** Li You decides not to take a taxi because she thinks it is too expensive.

( ) **4.** Li You doesn't know how to get to the airport by means of public transportation.

( ) **5.** In order to get to the airport, Li You can take the subway first, then the bus.

( ) **6.** Li You finally agrees to go to the airport in Wang Peng's car.

B. Workbook Dialogue (True/False)

( ) **1.** The woman decided to go home for the winter break.

( ) **2.** The man invited the woman to visit his home.

( ) **3.** The man and the woman would drive to the man's home together.

( ) **4.** Airline tickets were not expensive.

II. Speaking Exercises

A. Answer the questions in Chinese based on the Textbook Dialogue. (INTERPRETIVE AND PRESENTATIONAL)

1. What was Li You going to do for the winter vacation?

2. What were the two modes of transportation that Li You considered in the beginning?

3. Why did Li You abandon her first two choices?

4. How did Li You finally go to the airport?

B. You and your partner participate in a simulated conversation. Ask each other's plans for the winter break, and which means of transportation you plan to take. (INTERPERSONAL)

C. Ask your partner the best way to get to the airport from his/her home and if there are any other alternatives. (INTERPERSONAL)

III. Reading Comprehension (INTERPRETIVE)

A. Read the following note and answer the questions. (True/False)

小李：

　　明天是我的生日，你明天到我家来吃晚饭，怎么样？到我家来你可以坐四路公共汽车，也可以坐地铁，都很方便。坐公共汽车慢，可是不用换车。坐地铁快，但是得换车，先坐红线，坐三站，然后换蓝线，坐两站下车就到了。希望你能来！明天见。

小白

十二月五日下午三点

Questions:

( ) **1.**　Little Li wants to take Little Bai to dinner tomorrow.

( ) **2.**　To go to Little Bai's home, it is faster to take the subway than the bus.

( ) **3.**　Little Bai's home is neither on the bus line nor on the subway line.

( ) **4.**　Little Bai's birthday is December 5.

( ) **5.**　Little Bai does not expect her friend to drive tomorrow.

B. Read the following email message and answer the questions. (True/False)

　　小白，你好。我是小高。我昨天才知道你这个周末要去机场。你告诉王朋了，可是怎么没告诉我呢？你别坐公共汽车去机场。坐公共汽车不方便，也很慢。你得坐五站，还要换地铁，太麻烦了。我可以开车送你到机场去。我开车开得很好。你今天回宿舍以后给我打个电话，好吗？要是你的飞机票已经买了，我想知道你的飞机是几点的。好，再见。

Questions:

( ) **1.** Little Bai will go to the airport today.

( ) **2.** Wang Peng knows that Little Bai is going to the airport.

( ) **3.** According to Little Gao, the public transportation to the airport is not convenient.

( ) **4.** Little Gao considers himself a good driver.

( ) **5.** Little Gao asked Little Bai to wait for his phone call later today.

( ) **6.** Little Gao knows that Little Bai has already purchased her airplane ticket.

C. What tickets does this place sell?

IV. Writing and Grammar Exercises

A. When a piece of new information is mentioned, it becomes known information or the focus/topic in the following utterance. Let's practice.

EXAMPLES:

1: **A:** 你复习生词语法了吗？(yes)

   B: <u>生词语法我复习了。</u>

2: **A:** 我昨天看了一个外国电影。(I saw <u>that movie</u>, too.)

   B: <u>那个电影我也看了。</u>

1. **A:** 你做功课了没有？(yes)

   B: _____

2. **A:** 你喜欢不喜欢喝中国茶？(yes)

   B: _____

3. **A:** 老师给了他一枝笔。(He gave <u>that pen</u> to his friend.)

   B: _____

4. **A:** 我昨天去买了一双鞋。(I don't like <u>that pair</u>.)

   B: _____

5. **A:** 我今天认识了一个男孩子。(Everyone knows <u>that young man</u>.)

   B: _____

B. Fill in the blanks with 或者 or 还是.

1. 他正在写信_____写日记？

2. 你觉得坐地铁方便_____坐公共汽车方便？

3. 你想买蓝色的，黑色的，_____咖啡色的裤子？

4. 今天晚上我想练习发音_____复习语法。

5. 我想要一杯咖啡_____一瓶可乐。

C. Look at the visuals given and answer the questions using "先...再..." (INTERPERSONAL)

EXAMPLE: **A:** 李友今天上什么课？ **1.** **2.**

B: <u>她今天先上中文课，再上电脑课。</u>

1. A: 王朋周末想怎么玩儿？ **1.** **2.**

B: _____

2. A: 张老师明天得做什么？ **1.** **2.**

B: _____

3. A: 白英爱寒假怎么回家？ **1.** **2.**

B: _____

D. Let's practice how to make suggestions by using "还是...吧." (INTERPERSONAL)

EXAMPLE: **A:** 今天晚上没事儿，我们看电视，好吗？

（没意思，去跳舞）

B: 看电视没意思，我们还是去跳舞吧！

1. **A:** 这件黑色的衬衫很便宜。我想买。（样子不好，别买）

   B: _____

2. **A:** 我想坐公共汽车去机场。（太麻烦，打车）

   B: _____

3. **A:** 我们今天晚上去听音乐会，怎么样？（没空，明天晚上）

   B: _____

E. Translate the following exchanges into Chinese. (PRESENTATIONAL)

1. **A:** How are we going to get to the airport? By taxi or subway?

   _____

   B: Taxi or subway both are okay.

   _____

2. **A:** Give me a ride to school tomorrow, all right?

   _____

   B: Sorry, I am very busy tomorrow. You'd better take the bus.

   _____

3. **A:** I am flying home this winter break.

   _____

   B: Did you get <u>the ticket</u>?

   _____

A: I got <u>the ticket</u> already. It's (a ticket) for December 15.

_____

B: On that day, we will have dinner first, and then I'll give you a ride to the airport.

_____

A: Really? That will be great. Thank you.

_____

B: Don't mention it.

_____

F. Little Wang is going to the airport by subway. Describe how he plans to get there from school based on the illustrations. (PRESENTATIONAL)

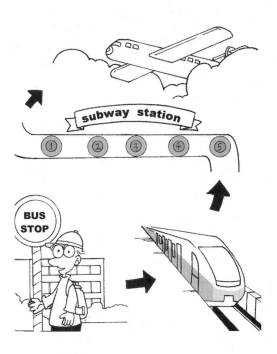

G. It's Little Wang's first time taking the Beijing subway. Little Wang is now at the Xizhimen (西直门) station. He has to go to Wangfujing (王府井) to do some shopping. Give him detailed directions based on this subway map. The names of the stations can be written in *pinyin*. To see a color version of the subway map, you can refer to Lesson 10 in the textbook or visit the companion website at **my.cheng-tsui.com**. (PRESENTATIONAL)

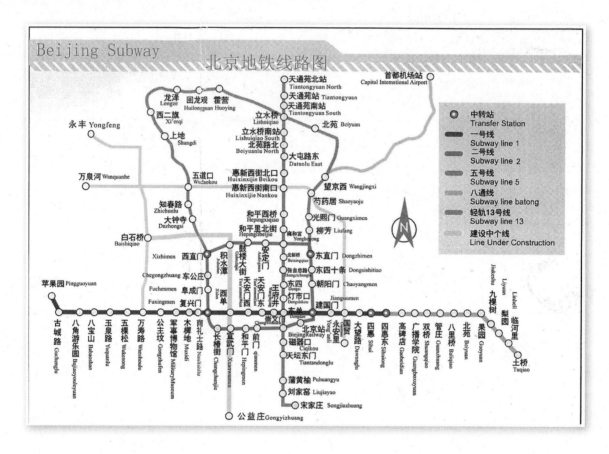

PART TWO An Email: Thanking Someone for a Ride

I. Listening Comprehension (INTERPRETIVE)

A. The Textbook E-mail (True/False)

( ) **1.** Wang Peng gave Li You a ride to the airport.

( ) **2.** Li You cannot drive.

( ) **3.** There is bus service but no subway in Li You's hometown.

( ) **4.** Li You was busy visiting old friends.

( ) **5.** Li You felt that everybody drove too slowly.

( ) **6.** Li You looked forward to hearing from Wang Peng.

B. Workbook Dialogue

( ) **1.** The woman knew how to get to the man's home.

( ) **2.** To get to the man's home by subway, one must first take the Green Line, then change to the Blue Line.

( ) **3.** The woman needs to take three different buses to get to the man's house.

( ) **4.** The woman decides to go to the man's place by bus.

C. Workbook Dialogue II

( ) **1.** The man would be busy the next day.

( ) **2.** The man claimed that he was a decent driver.

( ) **3.** The man would go to the airport with the woman.

( ) **4.** The woman didn't have total confidence in the man.

II. Speaking Exercises

A. Answer the questions in Chinese based on the e-mail in the textbook. (INTERPRETIVE AND PRESENTATIONAL)

1. How do you express New Year's greetings in Chinese?

2. Why did Li You thank Wang Peng?

3. What did Li You do for the past few days?

4. Was Li You a good driver? Please explain.

B. With a partner, do a role play. Call your friend and thank him/her for the ride to the airport. Tell him/her what you have been doing since you returned home, and wish your friend a happy New Year. (INTERPERSONAL)

C. Explain how to get to the airport from your friend's house by referring to the picture below. (PRESENTATIONAL)

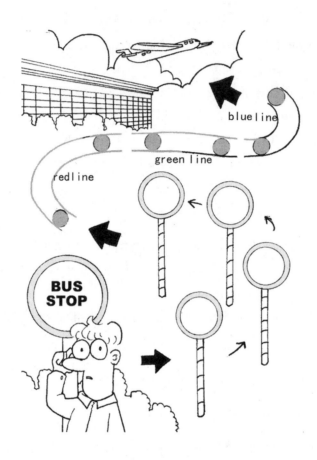

III. Reading Comprehension (INTERPRETIVE)

A. Read the following diary entry and answer the questions. (True/False)

小李的一篇日记

今天我开车去小张家找他玩儿。高速公路上的汽车很多，都开得很快。我不知道小张家怎么走，就给小张打手机，小张告诉我怎么走，可是因为在高速公路上开车让我很紧张，所以我开车开得特别慢，很晚才到小张家。

Questions:

( ) **1.** Little Li visited Little Zhang because they wanted to study together.

( ) **2.** Little Li was a skilled driver on highways.

( ) **3.** Little Li had no difficulties finding Little Zhang's place.

( ) **4.** Little Li probably was grateful that she had her cell phone with her.

( ) **6.** Little Li got to Little Zhang's place late because her car was too old.

B. Read the following passage and answer the questions. (True/False)

弟弟今天开车送妈妈去机场。高速公路上汽车很多，开得都很快，弟弟很紧张，所以开得特别慢。妈妈的飞机是两点半的，可是他们三点才到机场。机场的人告诉妈妈，她只能坐明天的飞机。弟弟很不好意思。他说明天再开车送妈妈去机场吧。可是妈妈说她明天还是自己坐出租汽车吧。

Questions:

( ) **1.** The brother is a very experienced driver.

( ) **2.** The traffic on the highway was light, so people drove fast.

( ) **3.** The brother drove very slowly because he was nervous.

( ) **4.** When they arrived at the airport, the mother's flight had departed.

( ) **5.** There were later flights today, but the mother preferred to wait until tomorrow.

( ) **6.** Most likely the mother will not ride in the same car to the airport tomorrow.

C. Read the following passage and answer the questions in English.

在中国，小孩都特别喜欢中国新年，因为他们可以穿新衣，穿新鞋，爸爸妈妈也给他们钱。不过，李小红告诉我她不喜欢中国新年。她三十岁，有先生，可是没有孩子，所以别人不给她钱，她还得给别人的小孩很多钱。李小红还说新年的时候公共汽车很少，她自己也没有车，所以出去玩也不方便。她觉得中国新年太没意思了。

1. What are the two things during Chinese New Year that make children so happy? Explain in detail.

_____

2. What are the two things during Chinese New Year that make Li Xiaohong unhappy? Explain in detail.

_____

_____

3. Is Li Xiaohong male or female? How do you know?

_____

D. This is the information on how to get to a theme park. Identify at least three means of transportation that can take tourists to the theme park.

_____

> **自行开车**
> 花莲县寿丰乡台11线10公里处。
>
> **飞　　机**
> 台北　远东、复兴航空公司，
> 航程约35分钟。
> 台中　华信航空公司，航程约1小时。
> 高雄　远东、华信航空公司，
> 航程约 50分钟。
>
> **铁　　路**
> 台北　观光列车由台北专车之达
> 花莲新站，约需3小时半。
> 台中　经由台北转由北回铁路直达。
> 高雄　经南回铁路由东部干线北上抵达。
>
> **公　　路**
> 大有巴士客运专车直达花莲市区后，
> 转搭花莲客运往台东、丰滨方向。
>
> **市区公车**
> 花莲港火车站发车往台东方向经海岸线。

IV. Writing and Grammar Exercises

A. What or who would make you nervous? Let's look at the visuals below, and write what makes Li You nervous. (PRESENTATIONAL)

什么让李友紧张？

1.  → _____

2. → _____

3. → _____

B. Answer the following questions according to your own circumstances. (PRESENTATIONAL)

1. 什么让你紧张？_____

2. 什么让你高兴？_____

3. 什么让你不好意思？_____

C. Answer the following questions with 每...都... (INTERPERSONAL)

EXAMPLE: **A:** 他<u>晚上</u>看电视吗？ **B:** <u>他每天晚上都看电视</u>。

1. **A:** 她<u>早上</u>走高速公路吗？ **B:** _____

2. **A:** 考试的时候<u>哪一个学生</u>很紧张？ **B:** _____

3. **A:** 常老师<u>哪个周末</u>回家？ **B:** _____

4. **A:** 那个商店的<u>什么衣服</u>很贵？ **B:** _____

D. Translate the following exchanges into Chinese. (PRESENTATIONAL)

1. **A:** You speak Chinese so well. Normally, how do you prepare for your Chinese class?

_____

_____

B: I listen to the audio every morning.

_____

2. **A:** We'll have dinner first, then we'll go dancing. My treat!

_____

_____

B: I feel bad about making you spend money.

_____

3. **A:** I'll give you a ride to school today.

_____

B: Never mind. I'd better take the bus.

_____

A: Why?

_____

B: You drive too fast, and it makes me nervous.

_____

A: Is that so?

_____

4. **A:** I like New York. This city is so interesting.

_____

B: I also think New York is quite nice. Its subway is especially convenient.

_____

_____

5. **A:** Do you know how to write e-mail messages in Chinese?

_____

B: Yes. I also know how to use a cell phone to write emails.

_____

A: Really? You're so cool.

_____

B: Everybody knows. You will be cool too if I teach you.

_____

A: Great! New Year is coming. I want to e-mail my friends and wish them a happy New Year.

_____

_____

B: Okay, I'll teach you now.

_____

E. Comment on how you drive, and how you drive on the highway. If you don't drive, comment on how people drive in your city or the public transportation in your city. (PRESENTATIONAL)

F. The holiday season is approaching. E-mail or text-message your friends in Chinese. Ask them how they are doing and wish them a happy New Year. (PRESENTATIONAL)

Let's Review (LESSONS 6–10)

I. How do we say these words?

Write down their correct pronunciation and tones in *pinyin*.

1. 喜欢_____   希望_____

2. 告诉_____   高速_____

3. 听录音_____   换绿线_____

4. 多少钱_____   都是钱_____

5. 售货员_____   以前或者以后_____

II. Group the characters according to their radicals.

客　得　笔　慢　错　然　词　线　贵　衫　钱
澡　等　室　货　烦　宿　绿　让　很　练　紧　语　懂　衬
律　笑　员　第　铁　裤　汽　念　照　洗　试

Radicals   **Characters**

1. _____   _____

2. _____   _____

3. _____   _____

4. _____   _____

5. _____   _____

6. _____   _____

7. _____   _____

8. _____   _____

9. _____   _____

10. _____   _____

11. _____   _____

III. Which of the following verbs are VO compounds?

学习   知道   开会   写字   告诉

付钱   坐地铁   下车   说话   预习

IV. Survey! Survey! Survey! (INTERPERSONAL AND PRESENTATIONAL)

Survey 1: Academic Progress

Go around the classroom and ask your classmates the following questions. Jot down the information you gather, and report back to the class on who has the most in common with you.

你是大学几年级的学生？ _____

你的专业是什么？ _____

你这个学期上什么课？ _____

你每天有几节课？ _____

你最喜欢上什么课？ _____

你最不喜欢上什么课？ _____

你的考试多不多？ _____

你什么课考试考得最好？ _____

Survey 2: It's All about Chinese

Pair up with a classmate, and ask each other the following questions. Present an oral or written report to your class based on the information you collect.

你为什么学中文？ _____

你觉得学中文有意思吗？ _____

你常常跟谁一起练习说中文？ _____

你去老师的办公室问问题吗？ _____

你觉得每课的生词多不多？语法难不难？ _____

_____

你平常先听录音再练习汉字还是先练习汉字再听录音？ _____

_____

你平常上新课以前预习吗？ _____

你平常考试以前找谁帮你复习？ _____

你平常考试考得怎么样？ _____

你觉得你的老师说话说得快不快？ _____

你觉得你写汉字写得怎么样？ _____

你会不会用中文写信、写日记、或者写电子邮件？ _____

_____

Survey 3: The Perfect Gift

You are trying to find a birthday gift for your friend. Ask him/her the following questions and hopefully you'll find the perfect gift.

你希望有件新衬衫，有条新裤子，还是有双新鞋？ _____

_____

你（不）喜欢什么颜色？ _____

衬衫，你穿多大的？ _____

裤子，你穿几号的？鞋呢？ _____

你希望我自己去买，还是你跟我一起去买？ _____

_____

要是大小、长短不合适，你希望我帮你去商店换，还是你自己去

换？ _____

Survey 4: Driving

Before riding in a car with your friend, ask him/her the following questions.

你会开车吗？ _____

要是你昨天晚上没睡觉，你能开车吗？ _____

_____

你的车新不新？ _____

你开车开得怎么样？ _____

你常常一边开车、一边打手机吗？ _____

_____

你在高速公路上开车紧张不紧张？ _____

_____

要是开车的时候，你的车有问题，我们坐公共汽车还是打车？

_____